THE POETRY PLEASE!

BOOK OF
FAVOURITE POEMS

THE POETRY PLEASE!

BOOK OF FAVOURITE POEMS

A FURTHER SELECTION *of* POPULAR POEMS *from the* RADIO 4 SERIES

Edited by SUSAN ROBERTS

BBC BOOKS

This book is published to accompany the
radio series entitled *Poetry Please!*
Published by BBC Books,
a division of BBC Enterprises Limited,
Woodlands, 80 Wood Lane
London W12 0TT

First Published 1993
Compilation © BBC Books 1993
Introduction © Susan Roberts
Poems © Individual copyright holders (see page 158)

ISBN 0 563 36961 2

Set in 11/13 Garamond Roman by Ace Filmsetting Ltd, Frome
Printed and bound in Great Britain by Clays Ltd, St Ives Plc
Jacket printed by Belmont Press Ltd, Northampton

CONTENTS

7

INTRODUCTION

Poetry Please! was first broadcast in October 1979. The idea, a simple one (like many successful ideas for radio), for a programme of listeners' poetry requests was the late Brian Patten's. Brian invited a different poet each month to the studios in Bristol to introduce the selected poems. Since those early days, the programme has doubled in length from ten to twenty minutes, and now has a regular presenter, Simon Rae. Simon continues the tradition of introducing the requests, but each week he also talks to an invited guest, a poet, or, occasionally, a public figure with a known love of poetry. The programme also escapes from the studio from time to time, to take part in literary festivals and events up and down the country. *Poetry Please!* has become one of Radio Four's longest standing programmes, and even as it evolves, it remains a classic with a loyal, vocal audience, who send in over two hundred letters and requests a month.

Previous *Poetry Please!* anthologies have reflected listeners' tastes. Each contains a selection of the most popular poems measured by the number of requests. Along with the radio programme itself, the *Poetry Please!* books must represent the most democratic selections of poetry ever assembled! Although not all of the poems included can be described as great poetry, each one has communicated something particular to those who have taken the trouble to write in. It is this personal element which probably explains the popularity of one of the features of the new longer *Poetry Please!* – the guest's choice of a favourite poem. Even when poets are doing the choosing, the same personal note is important. Anthony Thwaite, for instance, says of his chosen poet, George Herbert, 'I'm not saying he's the greatest poet, but if pushed I would say he was my favourite.'

I have taken these favourite poems as the basis for this new *Poetry Please!* anthology, published to celebrate the programme's fifteenth anniversary. In addition, I have asked both the poets who presented the ten-minute programme, and the poetry readers who bring requested poems to life on air each week, to choose a poem. The result is a rich and unpredictable anthology, reflecting the tastes of over ninety contributors who have taken part in *Poetry Please!* since 1979.

Choosing a favourite poem is not always easy. 'Today's favourite poem is not tomorrow's – nor yesterday's!' John Fuller wrote, commenting on the difficulty of the task. Some poems are favoured simply for themselves. Others have played a more important part in the life of the person doing the choosing. Wendy Cope has had Carol Rumens' poem, 'Three Poets Play the Saké Cup Game' pinned to the notice board in her study for the last 10 years. She likes what the poem has to say about the writing of poetry. In her own work, Liz Lochhead is constantly drawn to the dramatic monologue and it is the intimacy of voice that Robert Lowell achieves in his fine example of the genre, 'To Speak of the Woe That is in Marriage' which attracts her to it. Matthew Sweeney has also chosen a poem that has influenced his own writing, 'The Last Words of my English Grandmother', by William Carlos Williams, whose voice, he thinks sounds so fresh, so contemporary, he can hardly believe the poem was written in 1920.

Some favourite poems have a strong effect on mood. Carol Ann Duffy says of Roy Fisher's poem 'Paraphrases': 'It makes me laugh a lot. It's about the plight of the poet and the very odd letters one can receive. Although exaggerated, it does contain a lot of truth.' Margaret Drabble, on the other hand, doesn't look to poetry to cheer her up. One of the reasons she gives for choosing William Wordsworth's 'Personal Talk', is that 'It has a sort of sorrowful mournful depth which I find deeply comforting.'

Then of course there are reasons associated as much with biographical factors as with personality. Alan Bennett admires Philip Larkin's 'MCMXLV'. It also strikes a particularly personal chord: 'I think the poem was suggested by an old photograph. It rings bells with me in that my mother had a brother called Clarence, and his photograph was always on the piano when I was a child. There must be thousands of families in the same situation with this mysterious figure of a man in an old-fashioned uniform around. He had been killed in the First War within three months, in particularly tragic circumstances in the sense that he had taken a relatively dangerous operation in order to enlist. In our family he was always regarded as a saint. It was a doubly unnecessary death which makes the First War seem much more tragic and unnecessary than anything which has happened since.'

But finally, what makes a poem – or a picture, or a piece of music – a personal favourite will always remain something of a mystery. As Simon Jenkins said about his chosen poet, 'I don't know quite why Edwin Muir has always appealed to me so much.' A favourite poem is simply one that gets under your skin, and I hope that, whether you're a regular listener to *Poetry Please!* or not, you will enjoy this fascinating selection. It may even provide you with some new favourite poems.

I would like to thank everyone who has contributed to this book, and everyone who has taken part in the programme over the years. *Poetry Please!* has had four producers during its 15 years: the late Brian Patten, Margaret Bradley, myself, and recently Julian Wilkinson. It's been a great privilege to work on what to my mind is an important and unique programme. Where else can you hear such a wide and diverse range of poetry, classic and contemporary, week after week? *Poetry Please!* may have changed a lot over the years, but the core of the programme remains the same – listeners' requests. Long may it continue. I raise a glass and drink a toast to the next 15 years.

Susan Roberts

13

Dannie Abse

PART OF PLENTY
by Bernard Spencer 1909–63

When she carries food to the table and stoops down
– Doing this out of love – and lays soup with its good
Tickling smell, or fry winking from the fire
And I look up, perhaps from a book I am reading
Or other work: there is an importance of beauty
Which can't be accounted for by there and then,
And attacks me, but not separately from the welcome
Of the food, or the grace of her arms.

When she puts a sheaf of tulips in a jug
And pours in water and presses to one side
The upright stems and leaves that you hear creak,
Or loosens them, or holds them up to show me,
So that I see the tangle of their necks and cups
With the curls of her hair, and the body they are held
Against, and the stalk of the small waist rising
And flowering in the shape of breasts;

Whether in the bringing of the flowers or the food
She offers plenty, and is part of plenty,
And whether I see her stooping, or leaning with the flowers,
What she does is ages old, and she is not simply,
No, but lovely in that way.

Fleur Adcock

GAME AFTER SUPPER
by Margaret Atwood 1939–

This is before electricity,
it is when there were porches.

On the sagging porch an old man
is rocking. The porch is wooden,

the house is wooden and grey;
in the living room which smells of
smoke and mildew, soon
the woman will light the kerosene lamp.

There is a barn but I am not in the barn;
there is an orchard too, gone bad,
its apples like soft cork
but I am not there either.

I am hiding in the long grass
with my two dead cousins,
the membrane grown already
across their throats.

We hear crickets and our own hearts
close to our ears;
though we giggle, we are afraid.

From the shadows around
the corner of the house
a tall man is coming to find us:

He will be an uncle,
if we are lucky.

John Agard

SPIRITS OF MOVEMENT
by James Berry 1924–

Surely, so alike, airborne wind gave birth
to water, issued the denser wash
and earthed the early offspring.

Inbuilt is wind-inheritance.
Rage of leaves resists face-wash
it's wind's arrival in trees.

Hear sea waves work-choir,
hear any waterfall wonder,
it's temple-roar of wind flooding woods.

A restless transparent busyness
going and going. Spirits of movement.
Both break all shores, mad mad in search.

Wind plays wild bands of ghosts.
Water organizes running river
and drives rain-floods hustling.

On any sitting duty
like being a pond or puddle,
canal or glassful

water waits to run away
or just disappear like wind.
In a settled state water is sad.

Drop a stone in a sleepy pool
you hear the sulk
of static water voiced.

Lock up water, give it time, it'll leave.
Drink it down, it presses wanting exit.
A job done, water vanishes.

Water'll freshen any body part
and be ready, hanging
in drips, to be off.

Does its work, yes. But to be
ungraspable, like wind,
water insists on its transfiguration.

Adjoa Andoh

A LITANY FOR SURVIVAL
by Audre Lorde 1934–92

For those of us who live at the shoreline
standing upon the constant edges of decision
crucial and alone
for those of us who cannot indulge
the passing dreams of choice
who love in doorways coming and going
in the hours between dawns
looking inward and outward
at once before and after
seeking a now that can breed
futures
like bread in our children's mouths
so their dreams will not reflect
the death of ours;

For those of us
who were imprinted with fear
like a faint line in the centre of our foreheads
learning to be afraid with our mother's milk
for by this weapon
this illusion of some safety to be found
the heavy-footed hoped to silence us
For all of us
this instant and this triumph
We were never meant to survive.

And when the sun rises we are afraid
it might not remain
when the sun sets we are afraid
it might not rise in the morning
when our stomachs are full we are afraid
of indigestion
when our stomachs are empty we are afraid
we may never eat again

when we are loved we are afraid
love will vanish
when we are alone we are afraid
love will never return
and when we speak we are afraid
our words will not be heard
nor welcomed
but when we are silent
we are still afraid.

So it is better to speak
remembering
we were never meant to survive.

Simon Armitage

THE DISCOVERY OF THE PACIFIC
by Thom Gunn 1929–

They lean against the cooling car, backs pressed
Upon the dusts of a brown continent,
And watch the sun, now Westward of their West,
Fall to the ocean. Where it led they went.

Kansas to California. Day by day
They travelled emptier of the things they knew.
They improvised new habits on the way,
But lost the occasions, and then lost them too.

One night, no-one and nowhere, she had woken
To resin-smell and to the firs' slight sound,
And through their sleeping-bag had felt the broken
Tight-knotted surfaces of the naked ground.

Only his lean quiet body cupping hers
Kept her from it, the extreme chill. By degrees
She fell asleep. Around them in the firs
The wind probed, tiding through forked estuaries.

And now their skin is caked with road, the grime
Merely reflecting sunlight as it fails.
They leave their clothes among the rocks they climb,
Blunt leaves of iceplant nuzzle at their soles.

Now they stand chin-deep in the sway of ocean,
Firm West, two stringy bodies face to face,
And come, together, in the water's motion,
The full caught pause of their embrace.

Kenneth Baker MP

THE SECRET PEOPLE
by G. K. Chesterton 1874–1936

Smile at us, pay us, pass us; but do not quite forget;
For we are the people of England, that never have spoken yet.
There is many a fat farmer that drinks less cheerfully,
There is many a free French peasant who is richer and sadder
    than we.
There are no folk in the whole world so helpless or so wise.
There is hunger in our bellies, there is laughter in our eyes;
You laugh at us and love us, both mugs and eyes are wet:
Only you do not know us. For we have not spoken yet.

The fine French kings came over in a flutter of flags and
    dames.
We liked their smiles and battles, but we never could say their
    names.
The blood ran red to Bosworth and the high French lords
    went down;
There was naught but a naked people under a naked crown.

And the eyes of the King's Servants turned terribly every way,
And the gold of the King's Servants rose higher every day.
They burnt the homes of the shaven men, that had been
    quaint and kind,
Till there was no bed in a monk's house, nor food that man
    could find.
The inns of God where no man paid, that were the wall of
    the weak,
The King's Servants ate them all. And still we did not speak.

And the face of the King's Servants grew greater than the
    King:
He tricked them, and they trapped him, and stood round him
    in a ring.

The new grave lords closed round him, that had eaten the
    abbey's fruits,
And the men of the new religion, with their bibles in their
    boots,
We saw their shoulders moving, to menace or discuss,
And some were pure and some were vile; but none took heed
    of us.
We saw the King as they killed him, and his face was proud
    and pale;
And a few men talked of freedom, while England talked of
    ale.

A war that we understood not came over the world and woke
Americans, Frenchmen, Irish; but we knew not the things they
    spoke.
They talked about rights and nature and peace and the
    people's reign:
And the squires, our masters, bade us fight; and scorned us
    never again.
Weak if we be for ever, could none condemn us then;
Men called us serfs and drudges; men knew that we were men.
In foam and flame at Trafalgar, on Albuera plains,
We did and died like lions, to keep ourselves in chains
We lay in living ruins; firing and fearing not
The strange fierce face of the Frenchmen who knew for what
    they fought,
And the man who seemed to be more than man we strained
    against and broke;
And we broke our own rights with him. And still we never
    spoke.

Our patch of glory ended; we never heard guns again.
But the squire seemed struck in the saddle; he was foolish, as
    if in pain.
He leaned on a staggering lawyer, he clutched a cringing Jew,

He was stricken; it may be, after all, he was stricken at
    Waterloo.
Or perhaps the shades of the shaven men, whose spoil is in
    his house,
Come back in shining shapes at last to spoil his last carouse:
We only know the last sad squires ride slowly towards the sea,
And a new people takes the land: and still it is not we.

They have given us into the hand of new unhappy lords,
Lords without anger and honour, who dare not carry their
    swords.
They fight by shuffling papers; they have bright dead alien
    eyes;
They look at our labour and laughter as a tired man looks at
    flies.
And the load of their loveless pity is worse than the ancient
    wrongs,
Their doors are shut in the evening; and they know no songs.

We hear men speaking for us of new laws strong and sweet,
Yet is there no man speaketh as we speak in the street.
It may be we shall rise the last as Frenchmen rose the first,
Our wrath come after Russia's wrath and our wrath be the
    worst.
It may be we are meant to mark with our riot and our rest
God's scorn for all men governing. It may be beer is best.
But we are the people of England; and we have not spoken
    yet.
Smile at us, pay us, pass us. But do not quite forget.

Jill Balcon

'HOPE' IS THE THING WITH FEATHERS
by Emily Dickinson 1830–86

'Hope' is the thing with feathers –
That perches in the soul –
And sings the tune without the words –
And never stops – at all –

And sweetest – in the Gale – is heard –
And sore must be the storm –
That could abash the little Bird
That kept so many warm –

I've heard it in the chillest land –
And on the strangest Sea –
Yet, never, in Extremity,
It asked a crumb – of Me.

Elizabeth Bell

O PUG!

by Stevie Smith 1902–71

To the Brownes' pug dog, on my lap, in their car,
coming home from Norfolk.

O Pug, some people do not like you,
But I like you,
Some people say you do not breathe, you snore,
I don't mind,
One person says he is always conscious of your behind,
Is that your fault?

Your own people love you,
All the people in the family that owns you
Love you: Good pug, they cry, Happy pug,
Pug-come-for-a-walk.

You are an old dog now
And in all your life
You have never had cause for a moment's anxiety,
Yet,
In those great eyes of yours,
Those liquid and protuberant orbs,
Lies the shadow of immense insecurity. There
Panic walks.

Yes, yes, I know,
When your mistress is with you,
When your master
Takes you upon his lap,
Just then, for a moment,
Almost you are not frightened.

But at heart you are frightened, you always have been.
O Pug, obstinate old nervous breakdown,
In the midst of *so* much love,
And such comfort,
Still to feel unsafe and be afraid,

How one's heart goes out to you!

June Barrie

From A SHROPSHIRE LAD

by A. E. Housman 1859–1936

XL

Into my heart an air that kills
   From yon far country blows:
What are those blue remembered hills,
   What spires, what farms are those?

That is the land of lost content,
   I see it shining plain,
The happy highways where I went
   And cannot come again.

Alan Bennett

MCMXIV

by Philip Larkin 1922–85

Those long uneven lines
Standing as patiently
As if they were stretched outside
The Oval or Villa Park,
The crowns of hats, the sun
On moustached archaic faces
Grinning as if it were all
An August Bank Holiday lark;

And the shut shops, the bleached
Established names on the sunblinds,
The farthings and sovereigns,
And dark-clothed children at play
Called after kings and queens,
The tin advertisements
For cocoa and twist, and the pubs
Wide open all day;

And the countryside not caring:
The place-names all hazed over
With flowering grasses, and fields
Shadowing Domesday lines
Under wheat's restless silence;
The differently-dressed servants
With tiny rooms in huge houses,
The dust behind limousines;

Never such innocence,
Never before or since,
As changed itself to past
Without a word – the men
Leaving the gardens tidy,

The thousands of marriages
Lasting a little while longer:
Never such innocence again.

James Berry

NATURE

by H. D. Carberry 1921–89

We have neither Summer nor Winter
Neither Autumn nor Spring.

We have instead the days
When gold sun shines on the lush green canefields –
Magnificently.

The days when the rain beats like bullets on the roofs
And there is no sound but the swish of water in the gullies
And trees struggling in the high Jamaica winds.

Also there are the days when the leaves fade from off guango*
    trees
And the reaped canefields lie bare and fallow in the sun.

But best of all there are the days when the mango and the
    logwood blossom.

When the bushes are full of the sound of bees and the scent
    of honey,
When the tall grass sways and shivers to the slightest breath of
    air,

When the buttercups have paved the earth with yellow stars
And beauty comes suddenly and the rains have gone.

* *Guango: This is the usual name in Jamaica; more commonly known in other parts of the Caribbean as saman: '[Native name.] A tropical American tree of the bean family Pithecolobium saman, the pods of which are used as cattle fodder.' [New English Dictionary].*

Margaret Bradley

THE GOOD-MORROW
by John Donne 1572–1631

I wonder by my troth, what thou and I
Did, till we loved? were we not weaned till then?
But sucked on country pleasures, childishly?
Or snorted we in the seven sleepers' den?
'Twas so; but this, all pleasures fancies be.
If ever any beauty I did see,
Which I desired, and got, 'twas but a dream of thee.

And now good-morrow to our waking souls,
Which watch not one another out of fear;
For love all love of other sights controls,
And makes one little room an everywhere.
Let sea-discoverers to new worlds have gone,
Let maps to other, worlds on worlds have shown,
Let us possess one world, each hath one, and is one.

My face in thine eye, thine in mine appears,
And true plain hearts do in the faces rest;
Where can we find two better hemispheres
Without sharp North, without declining West?
What ever dies, was not mixed equally;
If our two loves be one, or thou and I
Love so alike that none do slacken, none can die.

Jean 'Binta' Breeze

MARRYSONG
by Dennis Scott 1939–

He never learned her, quite. Year after year
that territory, without seasons, shifted
under his eye. An hour he could be lost
in the walled anger of her quarried hurt
or turning, see cool water laughing where
the day before there were stones in her voice.
He charted. She made wilderness again.
Roads disappeared. The map was never true.
Wind brought him rain sometimes, tasting of sea –
and suddenly she would change the shape of shores
faultlessly calm. All, all was each day new:
the shadows of her love shortened or grew
like trees seen from an unexpected hill,
new country at each jaunty helpless journey.
So he accepted that geography, constantly strange.
Wondered. Stayed home increasingly to find
his way among the landscapes of her mind.

Diana Bishop

THE TREES ARE DOWN
by Charlotte Mew 1869–1928

– and he cried with a loud voice:
Hurt not the earth, neither the sea, nor the trees –
(Revelation.)

They are cutting down the great plane-trees at the end of the
    gardens.
For days there has been the grate of the saw, the swish of the
    branches as they fall,
The crash of the trunks, the rustle of trodden leaves,
With the 'Whoops' and the 'Whoas', the loud common talk,
    the loud common laughs of the men, above it all.

I remember one evening of a long past Spring
Turning in at a gate, getting out of a cart, and finding a large
    dead rat in the mud of the drive.
I remember thinking: alive or dead, a rat was a god-forsaken
    thing,
But at least, in May, that even a rat should be alive.

The week's work here is as good as done. There is just one
    bough
   On the roped bole, in the fine grey rain,
       Green and high
       And lonely against the sky.
        (Down now! –)
       And but for that,
       If an old dead rat
Did once, for a moment, unmake the Spring, I might never
    have thought of him again.

It is not for a moment the Spring is unmade to-day;
These were great trees, it was in them from root to stem:
When the men with the 'Whoops' and the 'Whoas' have
    carted the whole of the whispering loveliness away
Half the Spring, for me, will have gone with them.

It is going now, and my heart has been struck with the hearts
of the planes;
Half my life it has beat with these, in the sun, in the rains,
In the March wind, the May breeze,
In the great gales that came over to them across the roofs
from the great seas.
There was only a quiet rain when they were dying;
They must have heard the sparrows flying,
And the small creeping creatures in the earth where they were
lying –
But I, all day, I heard an angel crying:
'Hurt not the trees.'

Eleanor Bron

DOVER BEACH

by Matthew Arnold 1822–88

The sea is calm to-night.
The tide is full, the moon lies fair
Upon the straits; – on the French coast the light
Gleams and is gone; the cliffs of England stand,
Glimmering and vast, out in the tranquil bay.
Come to the window, sweet is the night-air!
Only, from the long line of spray
Where the sea meets the moon-blanched land,
Listen! you hear the grating roar
Of pebbles which the waves draw back, and fling,
At their return, up the high strand,
Begin, and cease, and then again begin,
With tremulous cadence slow, and bring
The eternal note of sadness in.

Sophocles long ago
Heard it on the Ægæan, and it brought
Into his mind the turbid ebb and flow
Of human misery; we
Find also in the sound a thought,
Hearing it by this distant northern sea.

The Sea of Faith
Was once, too, at the full, and round earth's shore
Lay like the folds of a bright girdle furled.
But now I only hear
Its melancholy, long, withdrawing roar,
Retreating, to the breath
Of the night-wind, down the vast edges drear
And naked shingles of the world.

Ah, love, let us be true
To one another! for the world, which seems
To lie before us like a land of dreams,

So various, so beautiful, so new,
Hath really neither joy, nor love, nor light,
Nor certitude, nor peace, nor help for pain;
And we are here as on a darkling plain
Swept with confused alarms of struggle and flight,
Where ignorant armies clash by night.

Alan Brownjohn

AT A WARWICKSHIRE MANSION
by Roy Fuller 1912–

Mad world, mad kings, mad composition
— King John

Cycles of ulcers, insomnia, poetry –
Badges of office; wished, detested tensions.
Seeing the parsley-like autumnal trees
Unmoving in the mist, I long to be
The marvellous painter who with art could freeze
Their transitory look: the vast dissensions
Between the human and his world arise
And plead with me to sew the hurt with eyes.

Horn calls on ostinato strings: the birds
Sweep level out of the umbrageous wood.
The sun towards the unconsidered west
Floats red, enormous, still. For these the words
Come pat, but for society possessed
With frontal lobes for evil, rear for good,
They are incongruous as the poisoner's
Remorse or as anaemia in furs.

In the dank garden of the ugly house
A group of leaden statuary perspires;
Moss grows between the ideal rumps and paps
Cast by the dead Victorian; the mouse
Starves behind massive panels; paths relapse
Like moral principles; the surrounding shires
Darken beneath the bombers' crawling wings.
The terrible simplifiers jerk the strings.

But art is never innocent although
It dreams it may be; and the red in caves
Is left by cripples of the happy hunt.
Between the action and the song I know

37

Too well the sleight of hand which points the blunt,
Compresses, lies. The schizophrenic craves
Magic and mystery, the rest the sane
Reject: what force and audience remain?

The house is dark upon the darkening sky:
I note the blue for which I never shall
Find the equivalent. I have been acting
The poet's role for quite as long as I
Can, at a stretch, without it being exacting:
I must return to less ephemeral
Affairs – to those controlled by love and power;
Builders of realms, their tenants for an hour.

John Carey

FOR ANDREW

by Fleur Adcock 1934–

'Will I die?' you ask. And so I enter on
The dutiful exposition of that which you
Would rather not know, and I rather not tell you.
To soften my 'Yes' I offer compensations –
Age and fulfilment ('It's so far away;
You will have children and grandchildren by then')
And indifference ('By then you will not care').
No need: you cannot believe me, convinced
That if you always eat plenty of vegetables
And are careful crossing the street you will live for ever.
And so we close the subject, with much unsaid –
This, for instance: Though you and I may die
Tomorrow or next year, and nothing remain
Of our stock, of the unique, preciously-hoarded
Inimitable genes we carry in us,
It is possible that for many generations
There will exist, sprung from whatever seeds,
Children straight-limbed, with clear enquiring voices,
Bright-eyed as you. Or so I like to think:
Sharing in this your childish optimism.

Charles Causley

THE FAITHLESS WIFE

by Federico Garcia Lorca 1899–1936

(Translated by Stephen Spender and J. L. Gili)

So I took her to the river
believing she was a maiden,
but she already had a husband.

It was on Saint James's night
and almost as if I was obliged to.
The lanterns went out
and the crickets lighted up.
In the farthest street corners
I touched her sleeping breasts,
and they opened to me suddenly
like spikes of hyacinth.
The starch of her petticoat
sounded in my ears
like a piece of silk
rent by ten knives.
Without silver light on their foliage
the trees had grown larger
and a horizon of dogs
barked very far from the river.

Past the blackberries,
the reeds and the hawthorn,
underneath her cluster of hair
I made a hollow in the earth.
I took off my tie.
She took off her dress.
I my belt with the revolver.
She her four bodices.
Nor nard nor mother-o'-pearl
have skin so fine,
nor does glass with silver

shine with such brilliance.
Her thighs slipped away from me
like startled fish,
half full of fire,
half full of cold.
That night I ran
on the best of roads
mounted on a nacre mare
without bridle or stirrups.
As a man, I won't repeat
the things she said to me.
The light of understanding
has made me most discreet.
Smeared with sand and kisses
I took her away from the river.
The swords of the lilies
battled with the air.

I behaved like what I am.
Like a proper gipsy.
I gave her a large sewing basket,
of straw-coloured satin,
and I did not fall in love
for although she had a husband
she told me she was a maiden
when I took her to the river.

Gillian Clarke

SALM I'R CREADURIAID
by Gwilym R. Jones 1903–

Dyrchafwn glod y bodau un-fantell
Sy'n fodlon ar eu cotiau blew a phlu,
A'r nofwyr na fynnant amgenach gwregys na'u crwyn.

Canwn
I'r morgrug na chyfrifant oriau eu diwydrwydd
Ar eu twmpath-fynyddoedd
Am fod fforest o glychau'r grug
Yn pereiddio'u llafur;
I'r genau-bo-gwirion sy'n ddoethach na dynion,
Ac i'r siani flewog sy'n igam-ogamu ar win cabatsen.

Cenfigennwn wrth
Y bili-dowcer sy'n ymdrochi yn lliwiau drud
Y machlud ar y môr;
Yr eog heulog ei hoen
A ŵyr sut i fagu cywion heb gardod;
Y ddylluan loer-feddw
Sy'n falch am fod nos tu draw i'r dydd,
A'r wiwer sy'n sleifio i Annwfn
I bendwmpian drwy'r hirlwm.

Eiliwn fawl
I adar y chwedlau,
Colomen Noe a drudwy Branwen
A fu'n postmona dros ddyfroedd,
Ac adar Rhiannon
A roddai nosweithiau llawen i'r meirw
A pheri i esgyrn ddawnsio.

Ac nac anghofiwn
Y clagwydd herciog
A roes ambell gwilsyn i'r Esgob Morgan,
Gan roddi nawdd ei esgyll i'r iaith Gymraeg,
A'r ieir-wragedd a gyweiriodd
Welyau Cymreig â'u gwres.

Translation

PSALM TO THE CREATURES
by Gwilym R. Jones 1903–

Let us celebrate the single-cloaked beings
Content in their coats of fur and feathers,
And the swimmers who wish no other garb than their skins.

Let us sing
The ants who do not reckon their hours of diligence
On their hillock-years
Because a forest of heather-bells
Sweetens their labour;
The common newt is wiser than men,
And the woolly-bear who zig-zags on cabbage wine.

Let us envy
The cormorant who bathes in the precious colours
Of sunset on the sea;
The salmon, sunny his bliss,
Who knows how to breed young without charity;
The moon-drunk owl
Proud because night is the other side of day,
And the squirrel who slinks to Annwfn
To doze away the long barren season.

Let us weave praise
For the birds of legends,
Noah's dove and Branwen's starling
Who carried the mail across the waters,
And Rhiannon's birds
Who gave merry nights to the dead
And caused bones to dance.

And let us not forget
The hopping gander
Who gave a few quills to Bishop Morgan,
Giving the haven of its wings to the Welsh language,
And the mother-hens who provided
Welsh beds with their warmth.

Ann Clwyd MP

From GWALIA DESERTA

by Idris Davies 1905–53

VIII

Do you remember 1926? That summer of soups and speeches,
The sunlight on the idle wheels and the deserted crossings,
And the laughter and the cursing in the moonlit streets?
Do you remember 1926? The slogans and the penny concerts,
The jazz-bands and the moorland picnics,
And the slanderous tongues of famous cities?
Do you remember 1926? The great dream and the swift
   disaster,
The fanatic and the traitor, and more than all,
The bravery of the simple, faithful folk?
'Ay, ay, we remember 1926,' said Dai and Shinkin,
As they stood on the kerb in Charing Cross Road,
'And we shall remember 1926 until our blood is dry.'

IX

When greed was born
In Monmouthshire,
The hills were torn
For Mammon's fire,
And wheels went round
And skulls were cracked,
And limbs were ground
And nerves were wracked.
No time to dream,
No time to stare,
In that fell scheme
To foul the air,
To grab the coal
And scorn the tree,

And sell the soul
To buy a spree.
And breasts were bruised
In dismal dens,
And streets were used
As breeding pens,
And babes were born
To feed the fire,
When hills were torn
In Monmouthshire.

Wendy Cope

THREE POETS PLAY THE SAKÉ CUP GAME
by Carol Rumens 1944–

A print dating from the Edo period shows a group of Japanese poets playing a game involving the floating of saké cups on a stream. One poet would launch the cup, and another, standing at a certain distance downstream, would try to compose a haiku by the time the cup reached him. In the print, the resulting poems are being hung to dry on the branches of a tree.

1

Tying his proud syllables
to a scented branch,
the poet hears laughter.
He turns and sees the cup
lodged winking in some reeds.
It will never pass him now.
As life begins, the poet muses,
so it stops, without warning.
Haiku is the game in the middle.
'Have I won?' he asks. 'Or lost?'

2

The orange saké cup
throbs on the bright stream
with petals, like a migraine.
It's only one word he wants,
one last, ripe cherry
brimming with the juice of his poem.
The cup weaves nearer. Demons
toss him a flashy adjective.
He sighs, and scribbles.
Sometimes, he can't bear to be a poet!

3

The idea grows.
He must be careful, careful.
Never mind the jeering,

winter's a difficult season
and this could be the truth.
He mustn't let it slip by
as the saké cup slips by.
When he wakes from the poem,
it's dark, the cherry has dropped
many leaves, his friends have gone.

Geoffrey Crellin

AT THE PLAY

by T. E. Brown 1830–97

As in a theatre the amuséd sense
Beholds the strange vicissitudes of things,
Young Damon's loves, the fates of clowns and kings,
And all the motley of the gay pretence –
Beholds, and on an acme of suspense
Stands vibrant till the curtain falls, door swings,
Lights gutter, and the weary murmurings
Of o'er-watched varlets intimate us thence:
Even so we gaze not on the things that are,
Nor aught behold but what is adumbrate.
The show is specious, and we laugh and weep
At what is only meant spectacular;
And when the curtain falls, we may not wait:
Death takes the lights, and we go home to sleep.

Kevin Crossley-Holland

THE OAK AND THE OLIVE
by George Barker 1913–

Seven years lived in Italy leave me convinced
that the angel guarding us knows only too well
what she is doing. There is a curious sense
in which that place whose floral sophistication
– whose moral sophistication – we all happily acknowledge,
resembles in fact a delicious garden inhabited
by seven-year-old children. I can perceive
this innocence of spirit even in the most cynical
of Italians I have loved, and I think that
this innocence ensues simply from the sun. There
it is perfectly possible to assassinate one's best friend
with a kind of histrionic guiltlessness, because
the sun would continue to shine after the crime,
the gardens to dream in the afternoon, and later
the evening cast a benevolent shadowing over
the corpse of one's cold friend. Furthermore years
of white and gold sunlight tend to deprive one of
the pessimistic faculty. It is harder to indulge there
the natural Anglosaxon melancholy
because I, for instance, found a bough of oranges
growing through the skylight of my lavatory.
And all these mother of pearl evenings and these
serene Venus green skies and Lucullan landscapes
have in the end the effect of depriving one
of precisely that consciousness of shame out
of which the adult Nordic monster
of evil is generated. There are no Grendls here.
And so it is possible often in the Borghese
Gardens to act as though one was, of course,
a criminal cynic but a criminal cynic whom
the sun does not decline to befriend, to whom small
birds still confide, and whom the sylvan
evening landscape is still prepared to sleep with.

49

Then it seems likely that Providence or Italy or
even the conscience has forgiven us the enormities
that brought us here. When the chilling
rain falls upon me in the North I know
only too well that it does so as

a moral punitive. I write this in
a Norfolk August and the rains pour down
daily upon a landscape which derives
its masculine nobility from the simple
fact that it has survived. It has survived
the flood, the winter, the fall and the Black
nor'-easter. The old oak tree hangs out
that great twisted bough from which the corpse
of the criminal cynic has just dropped in decay.
The clouds do not decorate the sky, they entomb it,
and the streams have swollen to cataracts. Weeds
flourish and the summer corn is crushed flat.
What could ever come from all this hopeless
melancholy save a knowledge, as by allegory,
of our culpability? Why, then, should I find
a child's face bright with tears haunting my mind?

Sorcha Cusack

THE FORGE

by Seamus Heaney 1939–

All I know is a door into the dark.
Outside, old axles and iron hoops rusting;
Inside, the hammered anvil's short-pitched ring,
The unpredictable fantail of sparks
Or hiss when a new shoe toughens in water.
The anvil must be somewhere in the centre,
Horned as a unicorn, at one end square,
Set there immoveable: an altar
Where he expends himself in shape and music.
Sometimes, leather-aproned, hairs in his nose,
He leans out on the jamb, recalls a clatter
Of hoofs where traffic is flashing in rows;
Then grunts and goes in, with a slam and flick
To beat real iron out, to work the bellows.

David Dabydeen

GOD'S GRANDEUR

by Gerard Manley Hopkins 1844–89

The world is charged with the grandeur of God.
    It will flame out, like shining from shook foil;
    It gathers to a greatness, like the ooze of oil
Crushed. Why do men then now not reck his rod?
Generations have trod, have trod, have trod;
    And all is seared with trade; bleared, smeared with toil;
    And wears man's smudge and shares man's smell: the soil
Is bare now, nor can foot feel, being shod.

And for all this, nature is never spent;
    There lives the dearest freshness deep down things;
And though the last lights off the black West went
    Oh, morning, at the brown brink eastward, springs –
Because the Holy Ghost over the bent
    World broods with warm breast and with ah! bright wings.

Fred D'Aguiar

HEARTEASE NEW ENGLAND 1987

by Lorna Goodison 1947–

I see a bird trapped
under the iron girders of the Ashmont station overpass.
It is trying to measure the distance between columns
with its given wing span, and it fails
for being alone and not having a wing span wide enough.
I am told that birds travel faster over greater distances
when they move in chevron formation
a group of birds could measure the width of the Ashmont
station overpass . . . I know how the bird feels.
I have come to see the backyards of the richest lands
on earth, their basements, their backrooms,
I have seen the poor asleep in carcasses of rooms.
Those who sleep together are fortunate
not to be one of the ultimate dispossessed
the truly homeless are usually alone
and tend to wakefulness.
In the fall I search for signs
a pattern in the New England flaming trees
'What is my mission? Speak, leaves'
(for all journeys have hidden missions)
The trees before dying, only flame brighter
maybe that is the answer, live glowing while you can.

That is the only answer, except one evening in November
I see an African in Harvard Square.
He is telling himself a story as he walks
in telling it, he takes all the parts
and I see that he has taken himself home.
And I have stories too, until I tell them
I will not find release, that is my mission.
Some nights though, anxiety assails me
a shroud spinning in the snow.
They say it's the affliction of this age,
it appears unasked, an unwelcome companion

53

who always wants you
to sit down and die with him
when for your own good you should keep going.
I know how the bird trying to measure the overpass feels.
I too can never quite get the measure of this world's structure
somewhere I belong to community, there
I am part of a grouping of many souls and galaxies
I am part of something ever evolving, familiar and most
   mighty.
I reaffirm this knowing one evening, a Wednesday
as I go up Shephard Street. Someone is playing
Bob Marley and the notes are levitating
across the Garden Street end of the street.
They appear first as notes and then feather into birds
pointing their wings, arranging themselves for travelling
long distances.
And birds are the soul's symbol, so I see
that I am only a sojourner here but I came as friend
came to record and sing and then, depart.
For my mission this last life is certainly this
to be the sojourner poet carolling for peace
calling lost souls to the way of Heartease.

Margaret Drabble

PERSONAL TALK

by William Wordsworth 1770–1850

I

I am not One who much or oft delight
To season my fireside with personal talk –
Of friends, who live within an easy walk,
Or neighbours, daily, weekly, in my sight;
And, for my chance-acquaintance, ladies bright,
Sons, mothers, maidens withering on the stalk,
These all wear out of me, like Forms with chalk
Painted on rich men's floors, for one feast-night.
Better than such discourse doth silence long,
Long, barren silence, square with my desire;
To sit without emotion, hope, or aim,
In the loved presence of my cottage-fire,
And listen to the flapping of the flame,
Or kettle whispering its faint undersong.

II

'Yet life,' you say, 'is life; we have seen and see,
And with a living pleasure we describe;
And fits of sprightly malice do but bribe
The languid mind into activity.
Sound sense, and love itself, and mirth and glee
Are fostered by the comment and the gibe.'
Even be it so: yet still among your tribe,
Our daily world's true Worldlings, rank not me!
Children are blest, and powerful; their world lies
More justly balanced; partly at their feet,
And part far from them: – sweetest melodies
Are those that are by distance made more sweet;
Whose mind is but the mind of his own eyes,
He is a Slave; the meanest we can meet!

III

Wings have we, – and as far as we can go
We may find pleasure: wilderness and wood,
Blank ocean and mere sky, support that mood
Which with the lofty sanctifies the low.
Dreams, books, are each a world; and books, we know,
Are a substantial world, both pure and good:
Round these, with tendrils strong as flesh and blood,
Our pastime and our happiness will grow.
There find I personal themes, a plenteous store,
Matter wherein right voluble I am,
To which I listen with a ready ear;
Two shall be named, pre-eminently dear, –
The gentle Lady married to the Moor;
And heavenly Una with her milk-white Lamb.

IV

Nor can I not believe but that hereby
Great gains are mine; for thus I live remote
From evil-speaking; rancour, never sought,
Comes to me not; malignant truth, or lie.
Hence have I genial seasons, hence have I
Smooth passions, smooth discourse, and joyous thought:
And thus from day to day my little boat
Rocks in its harbour, lodging peaceably.
Blessings be with them – and eternal praise,
Who gave us nobler loves, and nobler cares –
The Poets, who on earth have made us heirs
Of truth and pure delight by heavenly lays!
Oh! might my name be numbered among theirs,
Then gladly would I end my mortal days.

Carol Ann Duffy

PARAPHRASES
by Roy Fisher 1930–

for Peter Ryan

Dear Mr Fisher I am writing
a thesis on your work.
But am unable to obtain
texts. I have articles by Davie, D.,
and Mottram, E.,
but not your Books since booksellers
I have approached refuse to
take my order saying they
can no longer afford to
handle 'this type of business'. It is
too late! for me to change
my subject to the work of a more
popular writer, so please Mr Fisher
you must help me since I face the alternatives
of failing my degree or repaying
the whole of my scholarship money . . .

Dear Mr Fisher although I have been unable
to read much of your work (to get it that is)
I am a great admirer of it and your landscapes
have become so real to me I am convinced I have, in fact,
become you. I have never, however,
seen any photograph of you, and am most curious
to have an idea of your appearance,
beyond what my mirror, of course, tells me.
The cover of your *Collected Poems*
(reproduced in the *Guardian*, November 1971)
shows upwards of fifty faces; but which is yours? Are you
the little boy at the front, and if so have you
changed much since then?

Dear Mr Fisher recently while studying
selections from a modern anthology with
one of my GCE groups I came across your interestingly titled
'Starting to Make a Tree'. After the discussion I felt strongly
you were definitely *holding something back* in this poem
though I can't quite reach it. Are you often in Rugby?
If you are, perhaps we could meet and I could
try at least to explain. Cordially, Avis Tree. PS. Should we
arrange a rendezvous I'm afraid I wouldn't
know who to look out for as I've never unfortunately
seen your photograph. But I notice you were born in 1930
the same year as Ted Hughes. Would I be right
in expecting you to resemble *him*, more or less?

                                          – Dear Ms Tree,
It's true I'm in Rugby quite often, but the train
goes through without stopping. Could you fancy standing
outside the UP Refreshment Room a few times so that
I could learn to recognize *you*? If you could
just get hold of my four books, and wave them,
then I'd know it was you. As for my own appearance
I suppose it inclines more to the
Philip Larkin side of Ted Hughes's looks . . .
See if you think so as I go by . . .

Dear Mr Fisher I have been commissioned
to write a short
critical book on your work
but find that although I have a full
dossier of reviews etcetera
I don't have access to your books. Libraries
over here seem just not to have bought them in.
Since the books are quite a few years old now
I imagine they'll all have been remaindered
some while back? Or worse, pulped? So can
you advise me on locating second-hand copies,
not too expensively I hope? Anyway,

yours, with apologies and respect . . .

Dear Mr Fisher I am now
so certain I am you that it is obvious to me
that the collection of poems I am currently working on
                    must be
your own next book! Can you let me know –
who is to publish it and exactly when
it will be appearing? I shouldn't like there to
be any trouble over contracts, 'plagiarism'
etcetera; besides which it would be a pity
to think one of us was wasting time and effort.
How far have *you* got? Please help me. I
do think this is urgent . . .

Helen Dunmore

I HAVE THE PRESENT OF A BODY
by Osip Mandelstam 1892–1938

(Translated by David McDuff)

I have the present of a body – what should I do with it,
so indivisible it is and so much mine?

For the quiet joy of breathing and of being alive,
tell me, whom have I to thank?

I am the gardener and the flower,
in the dungeon of the world I am not alone.

On the panes of eternity has already settled
my breath, my warmth.

On it a pattern will print itself,
unrecognisable not long ago.

Let the lees of the moment trickle down –
the dear pattern is not to be wiped out.

Douglas Dunn

GOING BLIND
by Rilke 1875–1926

(Translated by Stephen Conn)

She sat there like the others at their tea:
I noticed first the curious way she seemed
to hold her cup – a little anxiously.
It almost hurt when, once, she gave a smile.

And when finally everybody rose
amid the talk and laughter – as we strolled
informally between the various rooms
I noticed her once more. She followed still

yet she seemed set apart – tense as a singer
who must soon appear before
her audience. The smiling eyes,
two pools reflecting back the light, were clear.

It seemed a hindrance must be overcome
and once that was achieved, transfigured, she
whose progress was so slow, so wearisome,
need never walk again, for she would fly.

Paul Durcan

THE PLEASANT JOYS OF BROTHERHOOD
by James Simmons 1933–

to the tune of 'My Lagan Love'

I love the small hours of the night
when I sit up alone.
I love my family, wife and friends.
I love them and they're gone.
A glass of Power's, a well-slacked fire,
I wind the gramophone.
The pleasant joys of brotherhood
I savour on my own.

An instrument to play upon,
books, records on the shelf,
and albums crammed with photographs:
I *céilí* by myself.
I drink to passion, drink to peace,
the silent telephone.
The pleasant joys of brotherhood
I savour on my own.

D. J. Enright

LOVE (3)
by George Herbert 1593–1633

Love bade me welcome: yet my soul drew back,
          Guilty of dust and sin.
But quick-eyed Love, observing me grow slack
          From my first entrance in,
Drew nearer to me, sweetly questioning,
          If I lacked anything.

A guest, I answered, worthy to be here:
          Love said, You shall be he.
I the unkind, ungrateful? Ah my dear,
          I cannot look on thee.
Love took my hand, and smiling did reply,
          Who made the eyes but I?

Truth Lord, but I have marred them: let my shame
          Go where it doth deserve.
And know you not, says Love, who bore the blame?
          My dear, then I will serve.
You must sit down, says Love, and taste my meat:
          So I did sit and eat.

Gavin Ewart

AUTOBIOGRAPHY
by Louis MacNeice 1907–63

In my childhood trees were green
And there was plenty to be seen.

Come back early or never come.

My father made the walls resound,
He wore his collar the wrong way round.

Come back early or never come.

My mother wore a yellow dress;
Gently, gently, gentleness.

Come back early or never come.

When I was five the black dreams came;
Nothing after was quite the same.

Come back early or never come.

The dark was talking to the dead;
The lamp was dark beside my bed.

Come back early or never come.

When I woke they did not care;
Nobody, nobody was there.

Come back early or never come.

When my silent terror cried,
Nobody, nobody replied.

Come back early or never come.

I got up; the chilly sun
Saw me walk away alone.

Come back early or never come.

U. A. Fanthorpe

THOUGHTS AFTER RUSKIN
by Elma Mitchell

Women reminded him of lilies and roses.
Me they remind rather of blood and soap,
Armed with a warm rag, assaulting noses,
Ears, neck, mouth and all the secret places:

Armed with a sharp knife, cutting up liver,
Holding hearts to bleed under a running tap,
Gutting and stuffing, pickling and preserving,
Scalding, blanching, broiling, pulverizing,
– All the terrible chemistry of their kitchens.

Their distant husbands lean across mahogany
And delicately manipulate the market,
While safe at home, the tender and the gentle
Are killing tiny mice, dead snap by the neck,
Asphyxiating flies, evicting spiders,
Scrubbing, scouring aloud, disturbing cupboards,
Committing things to dustbins, twisting, wringing,
Wrists red and knuckles white and fingers puckered,
Pulpy, tepid. Steering screaming cleaners
Arounds the snags of furniture, they straighten
And haul out sheets from under the incontinent
And heavy old, stoop to importunate young,
Tugging, folding, tucking, zipping, buttoning,
Spooning in food, encouraging excretion,
Mopping up vomit, stabbing cloth with needles,
Contorting wool around their knitting needles,
Creating snug and comfy on their needles.

Their huge hands! their everywhere eyes! their voices
Raised to convey across the hullabaloo,
Their massive thighs and breasts dispensing comfort,
Their bloody passages and hairy crannies,
Their wombs that pocket a man upside down!

And when all's over, off with overalls,
Quickly consulting clocks, they go upstairs,
Sit and sigh a little, brushing hair,
And somehow find, in mirrors, colours, odours,
Their essences of lilies and of roses.

James Fenton

LOBSTERS IN THE WINDOW

by W. D. Snodgrass 1926–

First, you think they are dead.
Then you are almost sure
One is beginning to stir.
Out of the crushed ice, slow
As the hands of a schoolroom clock,
He lifts his one great claw
And holds it over his head;
Now, he is trying to walk.

But like a run-down toy;
Like the backward crabs we boys
Splashed after in the creek,
Trapped in jars or a net,
And then took home to keep.
Overgrown, retarded, weak,
He is fumbling yet
From the deep chill of his sleep

As if, in a glacial thaw,
Some ancient thing might wake
Sore and cold and stiff
Struggling to raise one claw
Like a defiant fist;
Yet wavering, as if
Starting to swell and ache
With that thick peg in the wrist.

I should wave back, I guess.
But still in his permanent clench
He's fallen back with the mass
Heaped in their common trench
Who stir, but do not look out
Through the rainstreaming glass,
Hear what the newsboys shout,
Or see the raincoats pass.

John Fuller

CIRQUE D'HIVER

by Elizabeth Bishop 1911–79

Across the floor flits the mechanical toy,
fit for a king of several centuries back.
A little circus horse with real white hair.
His eyes are glossy black.
He bears a little dancer on his back.

She stands upon her toes and turns and turns.
A slanting spray of artificial roses
is stitched across her skirt and tinsel bodice.
Above her head she poses
another spray of artificial roses.

His mane and tail are straight from Chirico.
He has a formal, melancholy soul.
He feels her pink toes dangle toward his back
along the little pole
that pierces both her body and her soul

and goes through his, and reappears below,
under his belly, as a big tin key.
He canters three steps, then he makes a bow,
canters again, bows on one knee,
canters, then clicks and stops, and looks at me.

The dancer, by this time, has turned her back.
He is the more intelligent by far.
Facing each other rather desperately –
his eye is like a star –
we stare and say, 'Well, we have come this far.'

Garard Green

'CITIES AND THRONES AND POWERS'
by Rudyard Kipling 1865–1936

('A Centurion of the Thirtieth' – Puck of Pool's Hill)

Cities and Thrones and Powers
   Stand in Time's eye,
Almost as long as flowers,
   Which daily die:
But, as new buds put forth
   To glad new men,
Out of the spent and unconsidered Earth
   The Cities rise again.

This Season's Daffodil,
   She never hears
What change, what chance, what chill,
   Cut down last year's;
But with bold countenance,
   And knowledge small,
Esteems her seven days' continuance
   To be perpetual.

So Time that is o'er-kind
   To all that be,
Ordains us e'en as blind,
   As bold as she:
That in our very death,
   And burial sure,
Shadow to shadow, well persuaded, saith,
   'See how our works endure!'

Philip Gross

LIFE, FRIENDS, IS BORING
by John Berryman 1914–72

Life, friends, is boring. We must not say so.
After all, the sky flashes, the great sea yearns,
we ourselves flash and yearn,
and moreover my mother told me as a boy
(repeatingly) 'Ever to confess you're bored
means you have no

Inner Resources.' I conclude now I have no
inner resources, because I am heavy bored.
Peoples bore me,
literature bores me, especially great literature,
Henry bores me, with his plights & gripes
as bad as achilles,

who loves people and valiant art, which bores me.
And the tranquil hills, & gin, look like a drag
and somehow a dog
has taken itself & its tail considerably away
into mountains or sea or sky, leaving
behind: me, wag.

David Goodland

UP THERE

by Ivor Gurney 1890–1937

On Cotswold edge there is a field and that
Grows thick with corn and speedwell and the mat
Of thistles, of the tall kind; Rome lived there,
Some hurt centurion got his grant or tenure,
Built farm with fowls and pigsties and wood-piles,
Waited for service custom between whiles.
The farmer ploughs up coins in the wet-earth-time,
He sees them on the topple of crests gleam,
Or run down furrow; and halts and does let them lie
Like a small black island in brown immensity,
Till his wonder is ceased, and his great hand picks up the
    penny.
Red pottery easy discovered, no searching needed . . .
One wonders what farms were like, no searching needed,
As now the single kite hovering still
By the coppice there, level with the flat of the hill.

Dr John Habgood, Archbishop of York

PILGRIMAGES

by R. S. Thomas 1913–

There is an island there is no going
to but in a small boat the way
the saints went, travelling the gallery
of the frightened faces of
the long-drowned, munching the gravel
of its beaches. So I have gone
up the salt lane to the building
with the stone altar and the candles
gone out, and kneeled and lifted
my eyes to the furious gargoyle
of the owl that is like a god
gone small and resentful. There
is no body in the stained window
of the sky now. Am I too late?
Were they too late also, those
first pilgrims? He is such a fast
God, always before us and
leaving as we arrive.
                    There are those here
not given to prayer, whose office
is the blank sea that they say daily.
What they listen to is not
hymns but the slow chemistry of the soil
that turns saints' bones to dust,
dust to an irritant of the nostril.

There is no time on this island.
The swinging pendulum of the tide
has no clock; the events
are dateless. These people áre not
late or soon; they are just
here with only the one question

to ask, which life answers
by being in them. It is I
who ask. Was the pilgrimage
I made to come to my own
self, to learn that in times
like these and for one like me
God will never be plain and
out there, but dark rather and
inexplicable, as though he were in here?

Tony Harrison

TO HIS COY MISTRESS
by Andrew Marvell 1621–78

Had we but world enough, and time,
This coyness, Lady, were no crime.
We would sit down, and think which way
To walk, and pass our long love's day.
Thou by the Indian Ganges' side
Shouldst rubies find: I by the tide
Of Humber would complain. I would
Love you ten years before the flood:
And you should, if you please, refuse
Till the conversion of the Jews.
My vegetable love should grow
Vaster than empires, and more slow.
An hundred years should go to praise
Thine eyes, and on thy forehead gaze.
Two hundred to adore each breast:
But thirty thousand to the rest.
An age at least to every part,
And the last age should show your heart:
For, Lady, you deserve this state;
Nor would I love at lower rate.
　　But at my back I always hear
Time's wingèd chariot hurrying near:
And yonder all before us lie
Deserts of vast eternity.
Thy beauty shall no more be found;
Nor, in thy marble vault, shall sound
My echoing song: then worms shall try
That long-preserved virginity:
And your quaint honour turn to dust;
And into ashes all my lust.
The grave's a fine and private place,
But none, I think, do there embrace.

Now, therefore, while the youthful glue
Sits on thy skin like morning dew,
And while thy willing soul transpires
At every pore with instant fires,
Now let us sport us while we may;
And now, like amorous birds of prey,
Rather at once our time devour,
Than languish in his slow-chapped power.
Let us roll all our strength, and all
Our sweetness, up into one ball:
And tear our pleasures with rough strife,
Thorough the iron grates of life.
Thus, though we cannot make our sun
Stand still, yet we will make him run.

Denys Hawthorne

SANTA CLAUS IN A DEPARTMENT STORE
by Christopher Hassall 1912–63

Wolsey, or possibly my John of Gaunt,
Was the best thing I did. Come over here,
Behind the Christmas crib. (I'm not supposed
To let the children see me having tea.)
To tell the truth I'm glad of this engagement.
Dozens applied, but all they said was Thank you,
We'll stick to Mr. Borthwick.
It's nice to feel one has given satisfaction.
Time was I had it all at my finger-tips,
Could plant a whisper in the back of the pit,
Or hold them breathless with the authority
Of absolute repose – a skill despised,
Not seen, in *your* day. It amounts to this:
Technique's no more than the bare bones. There are some
Unwittingly instil the faith that Man
Is greater than he knows. This I fell short of.
    You never met my wife. You are too young.
She often came with me on tour. One night
At Nottingham, got back from the show, and there
She was. I knew at once what made her do it.
She had resented me for years. No, not
Myself, but what she knew was *in* me, my
Belief in – Sir, forgive me if I say
My 'art', for I had shown, you'll understand,
Some promise. To use her word, she felt herself
'Usurped', and by degrees, unconsciously,
She managed somehow to diminish me,
Parch all my vital streams. A look would do it.
I was a kind of shrunken river-bed
Littered with tins, old tyres, and bicycle frames.

Well, that was years ago, and by then too late
To start afresh. Yet all the while I loved her.
Explain that if you can. . . . By all means, madam,
Those clocks are very popular this year.
I'll call the man in charge. No, there's no risk
Of damage. They pack the cuckoo separately.

Adrian Henri

ENTER A CLOUD
by W. S. Graham 1918–

1

Gently disintegrate me
Said nothing at all.

Is there still time to say
Said I myself lying
In a bower of bramble
Into which I have fallen.

Look through my eyes up
At blue with not anything
We could have ever arranged
Slowly taking place.

Above the spires of the fox
Gloves and above the bracken
Tops with their young heads
Recognising the wind,
The armies of the empty
Blue press me further
Into Zennor Hill.

If I half-close my eyes
The spiked light leaps in
And I am here as near
Happy as I will get
In the sailing afternoon.

2

Enter a cloud. Between
The head of Zennor and
Gurnard's Head the long
Marine horizon makes
A blue wall or is it
A distant table-top
Of the far-off simple sea.

Enter a cloud. O cloud,
I see you entering from
Your west gathering yourself
Together into a white
Headlong. And now you move
And stream out of the Gurnard,
The west corner of my eye.

Enter a cloud. The cloud's
Changing shape is crossing
Slowly only an inch
Above the line of the sea.
Now nearly equidistant
Between Zennor and Gurnard's
Head, an elongated
White anvil is sailing
Not wanting to be a symbol.

3

Said nothing at all.

And proceeds with no idea
Of destination along
The sea bearing changing
Messages. Jean in London,
Lifting a cup, looking
Abstractedly out through
Her Hampstead glass will never
Be caught by your new shape
Above the chimneys. Jean,
Jean, do you not see
This cloud has been thought of
And written on Zennor Hill.

4

The cloud is going beyond
What I can see or make.
Over up-country maybe

Albert Strick stops and waves
Caught in the middle of teeling
Broccoli for the winter.
The cloud is not there yet.

From Gurnard's Head To Zennor
Head the level line
Crosses my eyes lying
On buzzing Zennor Hill.

The cloud is only a wisp
And gone behind the Head.
It is funny I got the sea's
Horizontal slightly surrealist.
Now when I raise myself
Out of the bracken I see
The long empty blue
Between the fishing Gurnard
And Zennor. It was a cloud
The language at my time's
Disposal made use of.

5

Thank you. And for your applause.
It has been a pleasure. I
Have never enjoyed speaking more.
May I also thank the real ones
Who have made this possible.
First, the cloud itself. And now
Gurnard's Head and Zennor
Head. Also recognise
How I have been helped
By Jean and Madron's Albert
Strick (He is a real man.)
And good words like brambles,
Bower, spiked, fox, anvil, teeling.

The bees you heard are from
A hive owned by my friend
Garfield down there below
In the house by Zennor Church.

The good blue sun is pressing
Me into Zennor Hill.

Gently disintegrate me
Said nothing at all.

Mick Imlah

From MAUD

by Alfred Lord Tennyson 1809–92

III

Cold and clear-cut face, why come you so cruelly meek,
Breaking a slumber in which all spleenful folly was drown'd,
Pale with the golden beam of an eyelash dead on the cheek,
Passionless, pale, cold face, star-sweet on a gloom profound;
Womanlike, taking revenge too deep for a transient wrong
Done but in thought to your beauty, and ever as pale as
    before
Growing and fading and growing upon me without a sound,
Luminous, gemlike, ghostlike, deathlike, half the night long
Growing and fading and growing, till I could bear it no more,
But arose, and all by myself in my own dark garden ground,
Listening now to the tide in its broad-flung ship-wrecking
    roar,
Now to the scream of a madden'd beach dragg'd down by the
    wave,
Walk'd in a wintry wind by a ghastly glimmer, and found
The shining daffodil dead, and Orion low in his grave.

Barbara Jefford

SONNET XXX

by William Shakespeare 1564–1616

When to the sessions of sweet silent thought
I summon up remembrance of things past,
I sigh the lack of many a thing I sought,
And with old woes new wail my dear times' waste:
Then can I drown an eye, unus'd to flow,
For precious friends hid in death's dateless night,
And weep afresh love's long since cancell'd woe,
And moan the expense of many a vanish'd sight:
Then can I grieve at grievances foregone,
And heavily from woe to woe tell o'er
The sad account of fore-bemoaned moan,
Which I new pay as if not paid before.
    But if the while I think on thee, dear friend,
    All losses are restor'd and sorrows end.

Peter Jeffrey

FIDELE'S GRASSY TOMB
by Sir Henry Newbolt 1862–1938

The Squire sat propped in a pillowed chair,
His eyes were alive and clear of care,
But well he knew that the hour was come
To bid good-bye to his ancient home.

He looked on garden, wood, and hill,
He looked on the lake, sunny and still:
The last of earth that his eyes could see
Was the island church of Orchardleigh.

The last that his heart could understand
Was the touch of the tongue that licked his hand:
'Bury the dog at my feet,' he said,
And his voice dropped, and the Squire was dead.

Now the dog was a hound of the Danish breed,
Staunch to love and strong at need:
He had dragged his master safe to shore
When the tide was ebbing at Elsinore.

From that day forth, as reason would,
He was named 'Fidele,' and made it good:
When the last of the mourners left the door
Fidele was dead on the chantry floor.

They buried him there at his master's feet,
And all that heard of it deemed it meet:
The story went the round for years,
Till it came at last to the Bishop's ears.

Bishop of Bath and Wells was he,
Lord of the lords of Orchardleigh;
And he wrote to the Parson the strongest screed
That Bishop may write or Parson read.

The sum of it was that a soulless hound
Was known to be buried in hallowed ground:
From scandal sore the Church to save
They must take the dog from his master's grave.

The heir was far in a foreign land,
The Parson was wax to my Lord's command:
He sent for the Sexton and bade him make
A lonely grave by the shore of the lake.

The Sexton sat by the water's brink
Where he used to sit when he used to think:
He reasoned slow, but he reasoned it out,
And his argument left him free from doubt.

'A Bishop,' he said, 'is the top of his trade;
But there's others can give him a start with the spade:
Yon dog, he carried the Squire ashore,
And a Christian couldn't ha' done no more.'

The grave was dug; the mason came
And carved on stone Fidele's name;
But the dog that the Sexton laid inside
Was a dog that never had lived or died.

So the Parson was praised, and the scandal stayed,
Till, a long time after, the church decayed,
And, laying the floor anew, they found
In the tomb of the Squire the bones of a hound.

As for the Bishop of Bath and Wells
No more of him the story tells;
Doubtless he lived as a Prelate and Prince,
And died and was buried a century since.

And whether his view was right or wrong
Has little to do with this my song;
Something we owe him, you must allow;
And perhaps he has changed his mind by now.

The Squire in the family chantry sleeps,
The marble still his memory keeps:
Remember, when the name you spell,
There rest Fidele's bones as well.

For the Sexton's grave you need not search,
'Tis a nameless mound by the island church:
An ignorant fellow, of humble lot –
But he knew one thing that a Bishop did not.

Alan Jenkins

THE FOX

by Paul Muldoon 1951–

Such an alarm
as was raised last night
by the geese
on John Mackle's goose-farm.

I got up and opened
the venetian blind.
You lay
three fields away

in Collegelands
graveyard, in ground
so wet you weren't so much
buried there as drowned.

That was a month ago.
I see your face
above its bib
pumped full of formaldehyde.

You seem engrossed,
as if I'd come on you
painfully writing your name
with a carpenter's pencil

on the lid
of a mushroom-box.
You're saying, **Go back to bed.
It's only yon dog-fox.**

Alan Jenkins

ROSE

by Ian Hamilton 1938–

In the delicately shrouded heart
Of this white rose, a patient eye,
The eye of love,
Knows who I am, and where I've been
Tonight, and what I wish I'd done.

I have been watching this white rose
For hours, imagining
Each tremor of each petal to be like a breath
That silences and soothes.
'Look at it', I'd say to you
If you were here: 'it is a sign
Of what is brief, and lonely
And in love.'

But you have gone and so I'll call it wise:
A patient breath, an eye, a rose
That opens up too easily, and dies.

Lord Jenkins of Hillhead

ANTICHRIST, OR THE REUNION OF CHRISTENDOM:
AN ODE

by G. K. Chesterton 1874–1936

'A Bill which has shocked the conscience of
every Christian community in Europe.'
– Mr. F. E. Smith, on the Welsh Disestablishment Bill.

Are they clinging to their crosses,
      F. E. Smith,
Where the Breton boat-flee tosses,
      Are they, Smith?
Do they, fasting, trembling, bleeding,
 Wait the news from this our city?
Groaning 'That's the Second Reading!'
 Hissing 'There is still Committee!'
If the voice of Cecil falters,
 If McKenna's point has pith,
Do they tremble for their altars?
      Do they, Smith?

Russian peasants round their pope
      Huddled, Smith,
Hear about it all, I hope,
      Don't they, Smith?
In the mountain hamlets clothing
 Peaks beyond Caucasian pales,
Where Establishment means nothing
 And they never heard of Wales,
Do they read it all in Hansard
 With a crib to read it with –
'Welsh Tithes: Dr. Clifford Answered.'
      Really, Smith?

In the lands where Christians were,
                        F. E. Smith,
In the little lands laid bare,
                        Smith, O Smith!
Where the Turkish bands are busy,
    And the Tory name is blessed
Since they hailed the Cross of Dizzy
    On the banners from the West!
Men don't think it half so hard if
    Islam burns their kin and kith,
Since a curate lives in Cardiff
                        Saved by Smith.

It would greatly, I must own,
                        Soothe me, Smith!
If you left this theme alone,
                        Holy Smith!
For your legal cause or civil
    You fight well and get your fee;

For your God or dream or devil
    You will answer, not to me.
Talk about the pews and steeples
    And the Cash that goes therewith!
But the souls of Christian peoples . . .
                        Chuck it, Smith!

Simon Jenkins

SONG

by Edwin Muir 1887–1959

Why should your face so please me
That if one little line should stray
Bewilderment would seize me
And drag me down the tortuous way
Out of the noon into the night?
But so, into this tranquil light
You raise me.

How could our minds so marry
That, separate, blunder to and fro,
Make for a point, miscarry,
And blind as headstrong horses go?
Though now they in their promised land
At pleasure travel hand in hand
Or tarry.

This concord is an answer
To questions far beyond our mind
Whose image is a dancer.
All effort is to ease refined
Here, weight is light; this is the dove
Of love and peace, not heartless love
The lancer.

And yet I still must wonder
That such an armistice can be
And life roll by in thunder
To leave this calm with you and me.
This tranquil voice of silence, yes,
This single song of two, this is
A wonder.

Jenny Joseph

A DIALOGUE BETWEEN THE SOUL AND BODY

by Andrew Marvell 1621–78

Soul

O who shall, from this dungeon, raise
A soul enslav'd so many ways?
With bolts of bones, that fettered stands
In feet; and manacled in hands.
Here blinded with an eye; and there
Deaf with the drumming of an ear.
A soul hung up, as 'twere, in chains
Of nerves, and arteries, and veins.
Tortured, besides each other part,
In a vain head, and double heart.

Body

O who shall me deliver whole,
From bonds of this tyrannic soul?
Which, stretched upright, impales me so,
That mine own precipice I go;
And warms and moves this needless frame:
(A fever could but do the same.)
And, wanting where its spite to try,
Has made me live to let me die.
A body that could never rest,
Since this ill spirit it possessed.

Soul

What magic could me thus confine
Within another's grief to pine?
Where whatsoever it complain,
I feel, that cannot feel, the pain.
And all my care its self employs,
That to preserve, which me destroys:
Constrained not only to endure

Diseases, but, what's worse, the cure:
And ready oft the port to gain,
Am shipwrecked into health again.

Body

But physic yet could never reach
The maladies thou me dost teach;
Whom first the cramp of hope does tear:
And then the palsy shakes of fear.
The pestilence of love does heat:
Or hatred's hidden ulcer eat.
Joy's cheerful madness does perplex:
Or sorrow's other madness vex.
Which knowledge forces me to know;
And memory will not forego.
What but a soul could have the wit
To build me up for sin so fit?
So architects do square and hew,
Green trees that in the forest grew.

P. J. Kavanagh

COCK-CROW

by Edward Thomas 1878–1917

Out of the wood of thoughts that grows by night
To be cut down by the sharp axe of light, –
Out of the night, two cocks together crow,

Cleaving the darkness with a silver blow:
And bright before my eyes twin trumpeters stand,
Heralds of splendour, one at either hand,
Each facing each as in a coat of arms:
The milkers lace their boots up at the farms.

Jackie Kay

TELEPHONE CONVERSATION
by Wole Soyinka 1934–

The price seemed reasonable, location
Indifferent. The landlady swore she lived
Off premises. Nothing remained
But self-confession. 'Madam,' I warned,
'I hate a wasted journey – I am African.'
Silence. Silenced transmission of
Pressurized good-breeding. Voice, when it came,
Lipstick coated, long gold-rolled
Cigarette-holder pipped. Caught I was, foully.
'HOW DARK?' . . . I had not misheard . . . 'ARE YOU LIGHT
OR VERY DARK?' Button B. Button A. Stench
Of rancid breath of public hide-and-speak.
Red booth. Red pillar-box. Red double-tiered
Omnibus squelching tar. It *was* real! Shamed
By ill-mannered silence, surrender
Pushed dumbfoundment to beg simplification.
Considerate she was, varying the emphasis –
'ARE YOU DARK? OR VERY LIGHT?' Revelation came.
'You mean – like plain or milk chocolate?'
Her assent was clinical, crushing in its light
Impersonality. Rapidly, wave-length adjusted,
I chose. 'West African sepia' – and as afterthought,
'Down in my passport.' Silence for spectroscopic
Flight of fancy, till truthfulness clanged her accent
Hard on the mouthpiece. 'WHAT'S THAT?' conceding
'DON'T KNOW WHAT THAT IS.' 'Like brunette.'
'THAT'S DARK, ISN'T IT?' 'Not altogether.
Facially I am brunette, but, madam, you should see
The rest of me. Palm of my hand, soles of my feet
Are a peroxide blond. Friction, caused –
Foolishly, madam – by sitting down, has turned
My bottom raven black – One moment, madam!' – sensing
Her receiver rearing on the thunderclap
About my ears – 'Madam,' I pleaded, 'wouldn't you rather
See for yourself?'

Elizabeth Kelly

AND SOME OF THE LARGER PIECES THAT YOU SEE ARE CALLED UNCLES

by Nigel Forde

for Fionn

A small, daily miracle; and you
are separate now.

Not separate enough to say
hallo to, but you've come
suddenly. You are.
As if to be were easy.

You lie in a loud tangle of birthdays.
Only one of them
your own.

Beside your cot is the world
we left there on the last night
before you were born. Now
it contains you. Elementary
metaphysics, and easy for
the finger of God, but some of us
like to be surprised by it still.

This is the world, then. It contains,
apart from you and me (and I
am one, according to Shelley,
of its unacknowledged legislators):
calves, that make far woodwind sounds
in brimming meadows; owls
that do the same thing after dark;
lupins, shoelaces, mineral deposits
and the Royal College of Heralds.
A variety of hats, sundials, people
who look a bit like someone else you know,

restored water-mills, presents
from Weston-super-Mare; hippopotamuses,
things with lids, lighthouses, gloves,
Reader's Digest Condensed Books,
things without lids, and one
Great Pyramid of Cheops.

Someone has also invented waves,
silk hayfields, music
and the considerate stars.
We're keeping them for you.

All of a sudden
I'm worried that you're not going
to like them.

There are things you can change.
Already your limbs stammer
as sharp as words. You've made
your first, tiny addendum
to the world's dictionary
as you take fistfuls of air
and squeeze them dry.

Liz Lochhead

TO SPEAK OF THE WOE THAT IS IN MARRIAGE
by Robert Lowell 1917–77

*'It is the future generation that presses into being by means of these exuberant feelings and
supersensible soap bubbles of ours.'*

Schopenhauer

'The hot night makes us keep our bedroom windows open.
Our magnolia blossoms. Life begins to happen.
My hopped up husband drops his home disputes,
and hits the streets to cruise for prostitutes,
free-lancing out along the razor's edge.
This screwball might kill his wife, then take the pledge.
Oh the monotonous meanness of his lust. . . .
It's the injustice . . . he is so unjust –
whiskey-blind, swaggering home at five.
My only thought is how to keep alive.
What makes him tick? Each night now I tie
ten dollars and his car key to my thigh. . . .
Gored by the climacteric of his want,
he stalls above me like an elephant.'

Michael Longley

INNOCENCE

by Patrick Kavanagh 1907–

They laughed at one I loved –
The triangular hill that hung
Under the Big Forth. They said
That I was bounded by the whitethorn hedges
Of the little farm and did not know the world.
But I knew that love's doorway to life
Is the same doorway everywhere.

Ashamed of what I loved
I flung her from me and called her a ditch
Although she was smiling at me with violets.

But now I am back in her briary arms
The dew of an Indian Summer morning lies
On bleached potato-stalks –
What age am I?

I do not know what age I am,
I am no mortal age;
I know nothing of women,
Nothing of cities,
I cannot die
Unless I walk outside these whitethorn hedges.

Roger McGough

STOPPING BY WOODS ON A SNOWY EVENING
by Robert Frost 1874–1963

Whose woods these are I think I know.
His house is in the village, though;
He will not see me stopping here
To watch his woods fill up with snow.

My little horse must think it queer
To stop without a farmhouse near
Between the woods and frozen lake
The darkest evening of the year.

He gives his harness bells a shake
To ask if there is some mistake.
The only other sound's the sweep
Of easy wind and downy flake.

The woods are lovely, dark, and deep,
But I have promises to keep,
And miles to go before I sleep,
And miles to go before I sleep.

Virginia McKenna

CAGED BIRD

by Maya Angelou 1928–

A free bird leaps
on the back of the wind
and floats downstream
till the current ends
and dips his wing
in the orange sun rays
and dares to claim the sky.

But a bird that stalks
down his narrow cage
can seldom see through
his bars of rage
his wings are clipped and
his feet are tied
so he opens his throat to sing.

The caged bird sings
with a fearful trill
of things unknown
but longed for still
and his tune is heard
on the distant hill
for the caged bird
sings of freedom.

The free bird thinks of another breeze
and the trade winds soft through the sighing trees
and the fat worms waiting on a dawn-bright lawn
and he names the sky his own.

But a caged bird stands on the grave of dreams
his shadow shouts on a nightmare scream
his wings are clipped and his feet are tied
so he opens his throat to sing.

The caged bird sings
with a fearful trill
of things unknown
but longed for still
and his tune is heard
on the distant hill
for the caged bird
sings of freedom.

Andrew Motion

REFERENCE BACK
by Philip Larkin 1922–85

That was a pretty one, I heard you call
From the unsatisfactory hall
To the unsatisfactory room where I
Played record after record, idly,
Wasting my time at home, that you
Looked so much forward to.

Oliver's *Riverside Blues*, it was. And now
I shall, I suppose, always remember how
The flock of notes those antique negroes blew
Out of Chicago air into
A huge remembering pre-electric horn
The year after I was born
Three decades later made this sudden bridge
From your unsatisfactory age
To my unsatisfactory prime.

Truly, though our element is time,
We are not suited to the long perspectives
Open at each instant of our lives.
They link us to our losses: worse,
They show us what we have as it once was,
Blindingly undiminished, just as though
By acting differently we could have kept it so.

Betty Mulchahy

THOUGHTS ABOUT THE PERSON FROM PORLOCK
by Stevie Smith 1902–71

Coleridge received the Person from Porlock
And ever after called him a curse,
Then why did he hurry to let him in?
He could have hid in the house.

It was not right of Coleridge in fact it was wrong
(But often we all do wrong)
As the truth is I think he was already stuck
With Kubla Khan.

He was weeping and wailing: I am finished, finished,
I shall never write another word of it,
When along comes the Person from Porlock
And takes the blame for it.

It was not right, it was wrong,
But often we all do wrong.

*

May we inquire the name of the Person from Porlock?

Why, Porson, didn't you know?
He lived at the bottom of Porlock Hill
So had a long way to go,

He wasn't much in the social sense
Though his grandmother was a Warlock,
One of the Rutlandshire ones I fancy
And nothing to do with Porlock,

And he lived at the bottom of the hill as I said
And had a cat named Flo,
And had a cat named Flo.
I am becoming impatient to see him
I think of him as a friend,

Often I look out of the window
Often I run to the gate
I think, He will come this evening,
I think it is rather late.

I am hungry to be interrupted
For ever and ever amen
O Person from Porlock come quickly
And bring my thoughts to an end.

*

I felicitate the people who have a Person from Porlock
To break up everything and throw it away
Because then there will be nothing to keep them
And they need not stay.

*

Why do they grumble so much?
He comes like a benison
They should be glad he has not forgotten them
They might have had to go on.

*

These thoughts are depressing I know. They are depressing,
I wish I was more cheerful, it is more pleasant,
Also it is a duty, we should smile as well as submitting
To the purpose of One Above who is experimenting
With various mixtures of human character which goes best,
All is interesting for him it is exciting, but not for us.
There I go again. Smile, smile, and get some work to do
Then you will be practically unconscious without positively
    having to go.

Paul Muldoon

DESIGN

by Robert Frost 1874–1963

I found a dimpled spider, fat and white,
On a white heal-all, holding up a moth
Like a white piece of rigid satin cloth –
Assorted characters of death and blight
Mixed ready to begin the morning right,
Like the ingredients of a witches' broth –
A snow-drop spider, a flower like a froth,
And dead wings carried like a paper kite.

What had that flower to do with being white,
The wayside blue and innocent heal-all?
What brought the kindred spider to that height,
Then steered the white moth thither in the night?
What but design of darkness to appall? –
If design govern in a thing so small.

Les Murray

TERRA AUSTRALIS
by James McAuley 1917–76

Voyage within you, on the fabled ocean,
And you will find that Southern Continent,
Quiros' vision – his hidalgo heart
And mythical Australia, where reside
All things in their imagined counterpart.

It is your land of similes: the wattle
Scatters its pollen on the doubting heart:
The flowers are wide-awake; the air gives ease.
There you come home; the magpies call you Jack
And whistle like larrikins at you from the trees.

There too the angophora preaches on the hillsides
With the gestures of Moses; and the white cockatoo,
Perched on his limbs, screams with demoniac pain;
And who shall say on what errand the insolent emu
Walks between morning and night on the edge of the plain?

But northward in valleys of the fiery Goat
Where the sun like a centaur vertically shoots
His raging arrows with unerring aim,
Stand the ecstatic solitary pyres
Of unknown lovers, featureless with flame.

Grace Nichols

LOT'S WIFE

by Anna Akhmatova 1889–1966

(Translated by Stanley Kunitz)

And the just man trailed God's shining agent,
over a black mountain, in his giant track,
while a restless voice kept harrying his woman:
'It's not too late, you can still look back

at the red towers of your native Sodom,
the square where once you sang, the spinning-shed,
at the empty windows set in the tall house
where sons and daughters blessed your marriage-bed.'

A single glance: a sudden dart of pain
stitching her eyes before she made a sound. . .
Her body flaked into transparent salt,
and her swift legs rooted to the ground.

Who will grieve for this woman? Does she not seem
too insignificant for our concern?
Yet in my heart I will never deny her,
she who suffered death because she chose to turn.

Ben Onwukwe

STRANGE MEETING
by Wilfred Owen 1893–1918

It seemed that out of battle I escaped
Down some profound dull tunnel, long since scooped
Through granites which titanic wars had groined.
Yet also there encumbered sleepers groaned,
Too fast in thought or death to be bestirred.
Then, as I probed them, one sprang up, and stared
With piteous recognition in fixed eyes,
Lifting distressful hands, as if to bless.
And by his smile, I knew that sullen hall, –
By his dead smile I knew we stood in Hell.
With a thousand pains that vision's face was grained;
Yet no blood reached there from the upper ground,
And no guns thumped, or down the flues made moan.
'Strange friend,' I said, 'here is no cause to mourn.'
'None,' said that other, 'save the undone years,
The hopelessness. Whatever hope is yours,
Was my life also; I went hunting wild
After the wildest beauty in the world,
Which lies not calm in eyes, or braided hair,
But mocks the steady running of the hour,
And if it grieves, grieves richlier than here.
For by my glee might many men have laughed,
And of my weeping something had been left,
Which must die now. I mean the truth untold,
The pity of war, the pity war distilled.
Now men will go content with what we spoiled,
Or, discontent, boil bloody, and be spilled.
They will be swift with swiftness of the tigress.
None will break ranks, though nations trek from progress.
Courage was mine, and I had mystery,
Wisdom was mine, and I had mastery:
To miss the march of this retreating world
Into vain citadels that are not walled.

Then, when much blood had clogged their chariot-wheels,
I would go up and wash them from sweet wells,
Even with truths that lie too deep for taint.
I would have poured my spirit without stint
But not through wounds; not on the cess of war.
Foreheads of men have bled where no wounds were.
'I am the enemy you killed, my friend.
I knew you in this dark: for so you frowned
Yesterday through me as you jabbed and killed.
I parried; but my hands were loath and cold.
Let us sleep now. . . .'

Gareth Owen

'BUFFALO BILL 'S'

by E. E. Cummings 1894–1962

Buffalo Bill 's
defunct
            who used to
            ride a watersmooth-silver
                                    stallion
and break onetwothreefourfive pigeonsjustlikethat
                                                Jesus

he was a handsome man
                        and what i want to know is
how do you like your blueeyed boy
Mister Death

Brian Patten

MY LAST DUCHESS

by Robert Browning 1812–89

FERRARA

That's my last Duchess painted on the wall,
Looking as if she were alive. I call
That piece a wonder, now: Frà Pandolf's hands
Worked busily a day, and there she stands.
Will't please you sit and look at her? I said
'Frà Pandolf' by design, for never read
Strangers like you that pictured countenance,
The depth and passion of its earnest glance,
But to myself they turned (since none puts by
The curtain I have drawn for you, but I)
And seemed as they would ask me, if they durst,
How such a glance came there; so, not the first
Are you to turn and ask thus. Sir, 'twas not
Her husband's presence only, called that spot
Of joy into the Duchess' cheek: perhaps
Frà Pandolf chanced to say 'Her mantle laps
Over my lady's wrist too much,' or 'Paint
Must never hope to reproduce the faint
Half-flush that dies along her throat:' such stuff
Was courtesy, she thought, and cause enough
For calling up that spot of joy. She had
A heart – how shall I say? – too soon made glad,
Too easily impressed; she liked whate'er
She looked on, and her looks went everywhere.
Sir, 'twas all one! My favour at her breast,
The dropping of the daylight in the West,
The bough of cherries some officious fool
Broke in the orchard for her, the white mule
She rode with round the terrace – all and each
Would draw from her alike the approving speech,
Or blush, at least. She thanked men, – good! but thanked

Somehow – I know not how – as if she ranked
My gift of a nine-hundred-years-old name
With anybody's gift. Who'd stoop to blame
This sort of trifling? Even had you skill
In speech – (which I have not) – to make your will
Quite clear to such an one, and say, 'Just this
Or that in you disgusts me; here you miss,
Or there exceed the mark' – and if she let
Herself be lessoned so, nor plainly set
Her wits to yours, forsooth, and made excuse,
– E'en then would be some stooping; and I choose
Never to stoop. Oh sir, she smiled, no doubt,
Whene'er I passed her; but who passed without
Much the same smile? This grew; I gave commands;
Then all smiles stopped together. There she stands
As if alive. Will't please you rise? We'll meet
The company below, then. I repeat,
The Count your master's known munificence
Is ample warrant that no just pretence
Of mine for dowry will be disallowed;
Though his fair daughter's self, as I avowed
At starting, is my object. Nay, we'll go
Together down, sir. Notice Neptune, though,
Taming a sea-horse, thought a rarity,
Which Claus of Innsbruck cast in bronze for me!

Ronald Pickup

DEATH BE NOT PROUD

by John Donne 1572–1631

X

Death be not proud, though some have called thee
Mighty and dreadful, for, thou art not so,
For, those, whom thou think'st, thou dost overthrow,
Die not, poor death, nor yet canst thou kill me.
From rest and sleep, which but thy pictures be,
Much pleasure, then from thee, much more must flow,
And soonest our best men with thee do go,
Rest of their bones, and soul's delivery.
Thou art slave to Fate, Chance, kings, and desperate men,
And dost with poison, war, and sickness dwell,
And poppy, or charms can make us sleep as well,
And better than thy stroke; why swell'st thou then?
One short sleep past, we wake eternally,
And death shall be no more, death, thou shalt die.

Tim Pigott-Smith

THE FARMER'S BRIDE
by Charlotte Mew 1869–1928

To –

He asked life of thee, and thou gavest him a long life:
even for ever and ever . . .

Three Summers since I chose a maid,
Too young maybe – but more's to do
At harvest-time than bide and woo.
   When us was wed she turned afraid
Of love and me and all things human;
Like the shut of a winter's day.
Her smile went out, and 'twasn't a woman –
   More like a little frightened fay.
      One night, in the Fall, she runned away.

'Out 'mong the sheep, her be,' they said,
'Should properly have been abed;
But sure enough she wasn't there
Lying awake with her wide brown stare.
So over seven-acre field and up-along across the down
   We chased her, flying like a hare
Before our lanterns. To Church-Town
   All in a shiver and a scare
We caught her, fetched her home at last
   And turned the key upon her, fast.

She does the work about the house
As well as most, but like a mouse:
   Happy enough to chat and play
   With birds and rabbits and such as they,
   So long as men-folk keep away.
'Not near, not near!' her eyes beseech
When one of us comes within reach.
   The women say that beasts in stall

115

Look round like children at her call.
I've hardly heard her speak at all.

Shy as a leveret, swift as he,
Straight and slight as a young larch tree,
Sweet as the first wild violets, she,
To her wild self. But what to me?

The short days shorten and the oaks are brown,
    The blue smoke rises to the low grey sky,
One leaf in the still air falls slowly down,
    A magpie's spotted feathers lie
On the black earth spread white with rime,
The berries redden up to Christmas-time.
    What's Christmas-time without there be
    Some other in the house than we!

    She sleeps up in the attic there
    Alone, poor maid. 'Tis but a stair
Betwixt us. Oh! my God! the down,
The soft young down of her, the brown,
The brown of her – her eyes, her hair, her hair!

Peter Porter

BEFORE LIFE AND AFTER

by Thomas Hardy 1840–1928

A time there was – as one may guess
And as, indeed, earth's testimonies tell –
　Before the birth of consciousness,
　　When all went well.

None suffered sickness, love, or loss,
None knew regret, starved hope, or heart-burnings;
　None cared whatever crash or cross
　　Brought wrack to things.

If something ceased, no tongue bewailed,
If something winced and waned, no heart was wrung;
　If brightness dimmed, and dark prevailed,
　　No sense was stung.

But the disease of feeling germed,
And primal rightness took the tinct of wrong;
　Ere nescience shall be reaffirmed
　　How long, how long?

Robert Powell

ODE TO THE WEST WIND
by Percy Bysshe Shelley 1792–1822

I

O Wild West Wind, thou breath of Autumn's being,
Thou, from whose unseen presence the leaves dead
Are driven, like ghosts from an enchanter fleeing,

Yellow, and black, and pale, and hectic red,
Pestilence-stricken multitudes: O thou,
Who chariotest to their dark wintry bed

The wingèd seeds, where they lie cold and low,
Each like a corpse within its grave, until
Thine azure sister of the Spring shall blow

Her clarion o'er the dreaming earth, and fill
(Driving sweet buds like flocks to feed in air)
With living hues and odours plain and hill:

Wild Spirit, which art moving everywhere;
Destroyer and preserver; hear, oh, hear!

II

Thou on whose stream, mid the steep sky's commotion,
Loose clouds like earth's decaying leaves are shed,
Shook from the tangled boughs of Heaven and Ocean,

Angels of rain and lightning: there are spread
On the blue surface of thine airy surge,
Like the bright hair uplifted from the head

Of some fierce Maenad, even from the dim verge
Of the horizon to the zenith's height,
The locks of the approaching storm. Thou dirge

Of the dying year, to which this closing night
Will be the dome of a vast sepulchre,
Vaulted with all thy congregated might

Of vapours, from whose solid atmosphere
Black rain, and fire, and hail will burst: oh, hear!

III

Thou who didst waken from his summer dreams
The blue Mediterranean, where he lay,
Lulled by the coil of his crystalline streams,

Beside a pumice isle in Baiae's bay,
And saw in sleep old palaces and towers
Quivering within the wave's intenser day,

All overgrown with azure moss and flowers
So sweet, the sense faints picturing them! Thou
For whose path the Atlantic's level powers

Cleave themselves into chasms, while far below
The sea-blooms and the oozy woods which wear
The sapless foliage of the ocean, know

Thy voice, and suddenly grow grey with fear,
And tremble and despoil themselves; oh, hear!

IV

If I were a dead leaf thou mightest bear;
If I were a swift cloud to fly with thee,
A wave to pant beneath thy power, and share

The impulse of thy strength, only less free
Than thou, O uncontrollable! If even
I were as in my boyhood, and could be

The comrade of thy wanderings over Heaven,
As then, when to outstrip thy skiey speed
Scarce seemed a vision; I would ne'er have striven

As thus with thee in prayer in my sore need.
Oh, lift me as a wave, a leaf, a cloud!
I fall upon the thorns of life! I bleed!

A heavy weight of hours has chained and bowed
One too like thee: tameless, and swift, and proud.

V

Make me thy lyre, even as the forest is:
What if my leaves are falling like its own!
The tumult of thy mighty harmonies

Will take from both a deep, autumnal tone,
Sweet though in sadness. Be thou, Spirit fierce,
My spirit! Be thou me, impetuous one!

Drive my dead thoughts over the universe
Like withered leaves to quicken a new birth!
And, by the incantation of this verse,

Scatter, as from an unextinguished hearth
Ashes and sparks, my words among mankind!
Be through my lips to unawakened earth

The trumpet of a prophecy! O, Wind,
If Winter comes, can Spring be far behind?

Elizabeth Proud

FARE WELL
by Walter de la Mare 1873–1956

When I lie where shades of darkness
Shall no more assail mine eyes,
Nor the rain make lamentation
  When the wind sighs;
How will fare the world whose wonder
Was the very proof of me?
Memory fades, must the remembered
  Perishing be?

Oh, when this my dust surrenders
Hand, foot, lip, to dust again,
May these loved and loving faces
  Please other men!
May the rusting harvest hedgerow
Still the Traveller's Joy entwine,
And as happy children gather
  Posies once mine.

Look thy last on all things lovely,
Every hour. Let no night
Seal thy sense in deathly slumber
  Till to delight
Thou have paid thy utmost blessing;
Since that all things thou wouldst praise
Beauty took from those who loved them
  In other days.

Simon Rae

THE LATEST DECALOGUE
by Arthur Hugh Clough 1819–61

Thou shalt have one God only; who
Would be at the expense of two?
No graven images may be
Worshipped, except the currency:
Swear not at all; for for thy curse
Thine enemy is none the worse:
At church on Sunday to attend
Will serve to keep the world thy friend:
Honour thy parents; that is, all
From whom advancement may befall:
Thou shalt not kill; but needst not strive
Officiously to keep alive:

Do not adultery commit;
Advantage rarely comes of it:
Thou shalt not steal; an empty feat,
When it's so lucrative to cheat:
Bear not false witness; let the lie
Have time on its own wings to fly:
Thou shalt not covet; but tradition
Approves all forms of competition.

The sum of all is, thou shalt love,
If any body, God above:
At any rate shall never labour
More than thyself to love thy neighbour.

Craig Raine

EPITHALAMION – A FRAGMENT
by Gerard Manley Hopkins 1844–89

Hark, hearer, hear what I do; lend a thought now, make
    believe
We are leafwhelmed somewhere with the hood
Of some branchy bunchy bushybowered wood,
Southern dean or Lancashire clough or Devon cleave,
That leans along the loins of hills, where a candycoloured,
    where a gluegold-brown
Marbled river, boisterously beautiful, between
Roots and rocks is danced and dandled, all in froth and
    waterblowballs, down.
We are there, when we hear a shout
That the hanging honeysuck, the dogeared hazels in the cover
Makes dither, makes hover
And the riot of a rout
Of, it must be, boys from the town
Bathing: it is summer's sovereign good.

By there comes a listless stranger: beckoned by the noise
He drops towards the river: unseen
Sees the bevy of them, how the boys
With dare and with downdolfinry and bellbright bodies
    huddling out,
Are earthworld, airworld, waterworld thorough hurled, all by
    turn and turn about.

This garland of their gambol flashes in his breast
Into such a sudden zest
Of summertime joys
That he hies to a pool neighbouring; see it is the best
There; sweetest, freshest, shadowiest;
Fairyland; silk-beech, scrolled ash, packed sycamore, wild
    wychelm, hornbeam fretty overstood
By. Rafts and rafts of flake leaves light, dealt so, painted on
    the air,

123

Hang as still as hawk or hawkmoth, as the stars or as the
    angels there,
Like the thing that never knew the earth, never off roots
Rose. Here he feasts: lovely all is! No more: off with – down
    he dings
His bleachèd both and woolwoven wear:
Careless these in coloured wisp
All lie tumbled-to; then with loop-locks
Forward falling, forehead frowning, lips crisp
Over finger-teasing task, his twiny boots
Fast he opens, last he off wrings
Till walk the world he can with bare his feet
And come where lies a coffer, burly all of blocks
Built of chancequarrièd, selfquainèd, hoar-huskèd rocks
And the water warbles over into, filleted with glassy grassy
    quicksilvery shivès and shoots
And with heavenfallen freshness down from moorland still
    brims,
Dark or daylight on and on. Here he will then, here he will
    the fleet
Flinty kindcold element let break across his limbs
Long. Where we leave him, froliclavish, while he looks about
    him, laughs, swims.

Enough now; since the sacred matter that I mean
I should be wronging longer leaving it to float
Upon this only gambolling and echoing-of-earth note –

What is . . . . the delightful dean?
Wedlock. What the water? Spousal love.

Christopher Reid

A TOCCATA OF GALUPPI'S

by Robert Browning 1812–89

I

Oh, Galuppi, Baldassaro, this is very sad to find!
I can hardly misconceive you; it would prove me deaf and
    blind;
But although I take your meaning, 'tis with such a heavy mind!

II

Here you come with your old music, and here's all the good it
    brings.
What, they lived once thus at Venice where the merchants
    were the kings,
Where St. Mark's is, where the Doges used to wed the sea
    with rings?

III

Ay, because the sea's the street there; and 'tis arched by . . .
    what you call
. . . Shylock's bridge with houses on it, where they kept the
    carnival:
I was never out of England – it's as if I saw it all!

IV

Did young people take their pleasure when the sea was warm
    in May?
Balls and masks begun at midnight, burning ever to mid-day
When they made up fresh adventures for the morrow, do you
    say?

V

Was a lady such a lady, cheeks so round and lips so red, –
On her neck the small face buoyant, like a bell-flower on its
    bed,
O'er the breast's superb abundance where a man might base
    his head?

VI

Well, (and it was graceful of them) they'd break talk off and
    afford
– She, to bite her mask's black velvet, he, to finger on his
    sword,
While you sat and played Toccatas, stately at the clavichord?

VII

What? Those lesser thirds so plaintive, sixths diminished, sigh
    on sigh,
Told them something? Those suspensions, those solutions –
    'Must we die?'
Those commiserating sevenths – 'Life might last! we can but
    try!'

VIII

'Were you happy?' – 'Yes.' – 'And are you still as happy?' –
    'Yes. And you?'
– 'Then, more kisses!' – 'Did *I* stop them, when a million
    seemed so few?'
Hark! the dominant's persistence, till it must be answered to!

IX

So an octave struck the answer. Oh, they praised you, I dare
    say!
'Brave Galuppi! that was music! good alike at grave and gay!
I can always leave off talking, when I hear a master play.'

X

Then they left you for their pleasure: till in due time, one by
    one,
Some with lives that came to nothing, some with deeds as well
    undone,
Death came tacitly and took them where they never see the
    sun.

XI

But when I sit down to reason, think to take my stand nor
    swerve,
While I triumph o'er a secret wrung from nature's close
    reserve,
In you come with your cold music, till I creep thro' every
    nerve.

XII

Yes, you, like a ghostly cricket, creaking where a house was
    burned –
'Dust and ashes', dead and done with, Venice spent what
    Venice earned!
The soul, doubtless, is immortal – where a soul can be
    discerned.

XIII

Yours for instance, you know physics, something of geology,
Mathematics are your pastime; souls shall rise in their degree;
Butterflies may dread extinction, – you'll not die, it cannot be!

XIV

As for Venice and its people, merely born to bloom and drop,
Here on earth they bore their fruitage, mirth and folly were
    the crop:
What of soul was left, I wonder, when the kissing had to
    stop?

XV

'Dust and ashes!' So you creak it, and I want the heart to
    scold.
Dear dead women, with such hair, too – what's become of all
    the gold
Used to hang and brush their bosoms? I feel chilly and grown
    old.

Christopher Ricks

I TO MY PERILS
by A. E. Housman 1859–1936

VI

I to my perils
   Of cheat and charmer
   Came clad in armour
     By stars benign.
Hope lies to mortals
   And most believe her,
   But man's deceiver
     Was never mine.

The thoughts of others
   Were light and fleeting,
   Of lovers' meeting
     Or luck or fame.
Mine were of trouble,
   And mine were steady,
   So I was ready
     When trouble came.

Tony Robinson

AS KINGFISHERS CATCH FIRE
by *Gerard Manley Hopkins 1844–59*

As kingfishers catch fire, dragonflies draw flame;
   As tumbled over rim in roundy wells
   Stones ring; like each tucked string tells, each hung bell's
Bow swung finds tongue to fling out broad its name;
Each mortal thing does one thing and the same:
   Deals out that being indoors each one dwells;
   Selves – goes itself; *myself* it speaks and spells,
Crying *What I do is me: for that I came.*

Í say more: the just man justices;
   Keeps gráce: thát keeps all his goings graces;
Acts in God's eye what in God's eye he is –
   Chríst. For Christ plays in ten thousand places,
Lovely in limbs, and lovely in eyes not his
   To the Father through the feature of men's faces.

Michael Rosen

THE COMMON AND THE GOOSE

Anonymous c. 1800

The law locks up the man or woman
Who steals the goose from off the common
But leaves the greater felon loose
Who steals the common from the goose.

Andrew Sachs

THE SISTERS

by Raymond Garlick 1926–

They shared the same house but did
Not speak, tried not to meet; hid
Their lives like pearls of great price –
The crochet, wireless news, rice
Puddings and so forth. Each had
Her personal door, was glad
To slam it – Miss Jones the back;
The widow would bivouac
Upstairs, and used the front. Two
Spry old women, sisters, who –
In a symbiotic game –
Stirred each other's lives aflame.

One fire died: Mrs Pritchard
Caught forever off her guard.
A son disposed of goods, cat.
Miss Jones said 'She won't like that' –
Impartially, as one who
Merely registered the view.
Two years later she claimed still
Her dustbin, nightly, would fill
With trash slipped round to *her* door.
Death is much less strong than war.

Vernon Scannell

DURING WIND AND RAIN
by Thomas Hardy 1840–1928

They sing their dearest songs –
He, she, all of them – yea,
Treble and tenor and bass,
    And one to play;
With the candles mooning each face. . . .
    Ah, no; the years O!
How the sick leaves reel down in throngs!

They clear the creeping moss –
Elders and juniors – aye,
Making the pathways neat
    And the garden gay;
And they build a shady seat. . . .
    Ah, no; the years, the years;
See, the white storm-birds wing across!

They are blithely breakfasting all –
Men and maidens – yea,
Under the summer tree,
    With a glimpse of the bay,
While pet fowl come to the knee. . . .
    Ah, no; the years O!
And the rotten rose is ript from the wall.

They change to a high new house,
He, she, all of them – aye,
Clocks and carpets and chairs
    On the lawn all day,
And brightest things that are theirs. . . .
    Ah, no; the years, the years;
Down their carved names the rain-drop ploughs.

Rosalind Shanks

MOUNTAIN LION

by D. H. Lawrence 1885–1930

Climbing through the January snow, into the Lobo canyon
Dark grow the spruce-trees, blue is the balsam, water sounds
    still unfrozen, and the trail is still evident.

Men!
Two men!
Men! The only animal in the world to fear!

They hesitate.
We hesitate.
They have a gun.
We have no gun.

Then we all advance, to meet.

Two Mexicans, strangers, emerging out of the dark and snow
    and inwardness of the Lobo valley.
What are they doing here on this vanishing trail?

What is he carrying?
Something yellow.
A deer?

Qué tiene, amigo?
León –

He smiles, foolishly, as if he were caught doing wrong.
And we smile, foolishly, as if we didn't know.
He is quite gentle and dark-faced.

It is a mountain lion,
A long, long slim cat, yellow like a lioness.
Dead.

He trapped her this morning, he says, smiling foolishly.
Lift up her face,
Her round, bright face, bright as frost.

Her round, fine-fashioned head, with two dead ears;
And stripes in the brilliant frost of her face, sharp, fine dark
    rays,
Dark, keen, fine rays in the brilliant frost of her face.
Beautiful dead eyes.

Hermoso es!

They go out towards the open;
We go on into the gloom of Lobo.
And above the trees I found her lair,
A hole in the blood-orange brilliant rocks that stick up, a little
    cave.
And bones, and twigs, and a perilous ascent.

So, she will never leap up that way again, with the yellow flash
    of a mountain lion's long shoot!
And her bright striped frost-face will never watch any more,
    out of the shadow of the cave in the blood-orange rock,
Above the trees of the Lobo dark valley-mouth!

Instead, I look out.
And out to the dim of the desert, like a dream, never real;
To the snow of the Sangre de Cristo mountains, the ice of the
    mountains of Picoris,
And near across at the opposite steep of snow, green trees
    motionless standing in snow, like a Christmas toy.

And I think in this empty world there was room for me and a
    mountain lion.
And I think in the world beyond, how easily we might spare a
    million or two of humans
And never miss them.
Yet what a gap in the world, the missing white frost-face of
    that slim yellow mountain lion!

Lobo.

Sir Stephen Spender

THEY FLEE FROM ME
by Sir Thomas Wyatt 1503–42

They flee from me that sometime did me seek,
    With naked foot stalking within my chamber:
Once have I seen them gentle, tame, and meek,
    That now are wild, and do not once remember
    That sometime they have put themselves in danger
To take bread at my hand; and now they range,
Busily seeking in continual change.

Thanked be fortune, it hath been otherwise
    Twenty times better; but once especial –
In thin array: after a pleasant guise,
    When her loose gown did from her shoulders fall,
    And she me caught in her arms long and small,
And therewithal so sweetly did me kiss,
And softly said, *'Dear heart, how like you this?'*

It was no dream; for I lay broad awaking:
    But all is turn'd now, through my gentleness,
Into a bitter fashion of forsaking;
    And I have leave to go of her goodness;
    And she also to use new-fangleness.
But since that I unkindly so am servèd,
'How like you this?' – what hath she now deservèd?

Anne Stevenson

SNOW

by Louis MacNeice 1907–63

The room was suddenly rich and the great bay-window was
Spawning snow and pink roses against it
Soundlessly collateral and incompatible:
World is suddener than we fancy it.

World is crazier and more of it than we think,
Incorrigibly plural. I peel and portion
A tangerine and spit the pips and feel
The drunkenness of things being various.

And the fire flames with a bubbling sound for world
Is more spiteful and gay than one supposes –
On the tongue on the eyes on the ears in the palms of one's
    hands –
There is more than glass between the snow and the huge
    roses.

Juliet Stevenson

THE CAP AND BELLS
by W. B. Yeats 1865–1939

The jester walked in the garden:
The garden had fallen still;
He bade his soul rise upward
And stand on her window-sill.

It rose in a straight blue garment,
When owls began to call:
It had grown wise-tongued by thinking
Of a quiet and light footfall:

But the young queen would not listen;
She rose in her pale night-gown;
She drew in the heavy casement
And pushed the latches down.

He bade his heart go to her,
When the owls called out no more;
In a red and quivering garment
It sang to her through the door.

It had grown sweet-tongued by dreaming
Of a flutter of flower-like hair;
But she took up her fan from the table
And waved it off on the air.

'I have cap and bells,' he pondered,
'I will send them to her and die';
And when the morning whitened
He left them where she went by.

She laid them upon her bosom,
Under a cloud of her hair,
And her red lips sang them a love-song
Till stars grew out of the air.

She opened her door and her window,
And the heart and the soul came through,

To her right hand came the red one,
To her left hand came the blue.

They set up a noise like crickets,
A chattering wise and sweet,
And her hair was a folded flower
And the quiet of love in her feet.

Matthew Sweeney

THE LAST WORDS OF MY ENGLISH GRANDMOTHER
by *William Carlos Williams 1883–1963*

There were some dirty plates
and a glass of milk
beside her on a small table
near the rank, disheveled bed –

Wrinkled and nearly blind
she lay and snored
rousing with anger in her tones
to cry for food,

Gimme something to eat –
They're starving me –
I'm all right I won't go
to the hospital. No, no, no

Give me something to eat
Let me take you
to the hospital, I said
and after you are well

you can do as you please.
She smiled, Yes
you do what you please first
then I can do what I please –

Oh, oh, oh! she cried
as the ambulance men lifted
her to the stretcher –
Is this what you call

making me comfortable?
By now her mind was clear –
Oh you think you're smart
you young people,

she said, but I'll tell you
you don't know anything.

Then we started.
On the way

we passed a long row
of elms. She looked at them
awhile out of
the ambulance window and said,

What are all those
fuzzy looking things out there?
Trees? Well, I'm tired
of them, and rolled her head away.

Stephen Thorne

anyone lived in a pretty how town
by E. E. Cummings 1894–1962

anyone lived in a pretty how town
(with up so floating many bells down)
spring summer autumn winter
he sang his didn't he danced his did.

Women and men(both little and small)
cared for anyone not at all
they sowed their isn't they reaped their same
sun moon stars rain

children guessed(but only a few
and down they forgot as up they grew
autumn winter spring summer)
that noone loved him more and more

when by now and tree by leaf
she laughed his joy she cried his grief
bird by snow and stir by still
anyone's any was all to her

someones married their everyones
laughed their cryings and did their dance
(sleep wake hope and then)they
said their nevers they slept their dream

stars rain sun moon
(and only the snow can begin to explain
how children are apt to forget to remember
with up so floating many bells down)

one day anyone died i guess
(and noone stooped to kiss his face)
busy folk buried them side by side
little by little and was by was

all by all and deep by deep

and more by more they dream their sleep
noone and anyone earth by april
wish by spirit and if by yes.

Women and men(both dong and ding)
summer autumn winter spring
reaped their sowing and went their came
sun moon stars rain

Anthony Thwaite

THE PEARL
Matthew 13:45

by George Herbert 1593–1633

I know the ways of learning; both the head
And pipes that feed the press, and make it run;
What reason hath from nature borrowed,
Or of itself, like a good huswife, spun
In laws and policy; what the stars conspire,
What willing nature speaks, what forc'd by fire;
Both th' old discoveries, and the new-found seas,
The stock and surplus, cause and history:
All these stand open, or I have the keys:
   Yet I love thee.

I know the ways of honour, what maintains
The quick returns of courtesy and wit:
In vies of favours whether party gains,
When glory swells the heart, and mouldeth it
To all expressions both of hand and eye,
Which on the world a true-love-knot may tie,
And bear the bundle, wheresoe'er it goes:
How many drams of spirit there must be
To sell my life unto my friends or foes:
   Yet I love thee.

I know the ways of pleasure, the sweet strains,
The lullings and the relishes of it,
The propositions of hot blood and brains;
What mirth and music mean; what love and wit
Have done these twenty hundred years, and more:
I know the projects of unbridled store:
My stuff is flesh, not brass; my senses live,
And grumble oft, that they have more in me
Than he that curbs them, being but one to five:
   Yet I love thee.

I know all these, and have them in my hand:
Therefore not sealed, but with open eyes
I fly to thee, and fully understand
Both the main sale, and the commodities;
And at what rate and price I have thy love;
With all the circumstances that may move:
Yet through the labyrinths, not my grovelling wit,
But thy silk twist let down from heaven to me;
Did both conduct, and teach me, how by it
    To climb to thee.

Charles Tomlinson

ON THE DEATH OF MRS THROCKMORTON'S
BULFINCH

by William Cowper 1731–1800

Ye nymphs! if e'er your eyes were red
With tears o'er hapless fav'rites shed,
   O share Maria's grief!
Her fav'rite, even in his cage,
(What will not hunger's cruel rage?)
   Assassin'd by a thief.

Where Rhenus strays his vines among,
The egg was laid from which he sprung,
   And though by nature mute,
Or only with a whistle blest,
Well-taught, he all the sounds express'd
   Of flagelet or flute.

The honours of his ebon poll
Were brighter than the sleekest mole;
   His bosom of the hue
With which Aurora decks the skies,
When piping winds shall soon arise
   To sweep up all the dew.

Above, below, in all the house,
Dire foe, alike to bird and mouse,
   No cat had leave to dwell;
And Bully's cage supported stood,
On props of smoothest-shaven wood,
   Large-built and lattic'd well.

Well-lattic'd – but the grate, alas!
Not rough with wire of steel or brass,
   For Bully's plumage sake,
But smooth with wands from Ouse's side,
With which, when neatly peel'd and dried,
   The swains their baskets make.

Night veil'd the pole – all seem'd secure –
When led by instinct sharp and sure,
    Subsistence to provide,
A beast forth-sallied on the scout,
Long-back'd, long-tail'd, with whisker'd snout,
    And badger-colour'd hide.

He, ent'ring at the study-door,
Its ample area 'gan explore;
    And something in the wind
Conjectur'd, sniffing round and round,
Better than all the books he found,
    Food, chiefly, for the mind.

Just then, by adverse fate impress'd,
A dream disturb'd poor Bully's rest;
    In sleep he seem'd to view
A rat, fast-clinging to the cage,
And, screaming at the sad presage,
    Awoke and found it true.

For, aided both by ear and scent,
Right to his mark the monster went –
    Ah, Muse! forbear to speak
Minute the horrors that ensued;
His teeth were strong, the cage was wood –
    He left poor Bully's beak.

He left it – but he should have ta'en
That beak, whence issued many a strain
    Of such mellifluous tone,
Might have repaid him well, I wote,
For silencing so sweet a throat,
    Fast set within his own.

Maria weeps – The Muses mourn –
So, when by Bacchanalians torn,
    On Thracian Hebrus' side

146

The tree-enchanter Orpheus fell;
His head alone remain'd to tell
  The cruel death he died.

John Whitworth

ON MY FIRST SON
by Ben Jonson 1572–1637

Farewell, thou child of my right hand, and joy;
　My sin was too much hope of thee, loved boy.
Seven years thou wert lent to me, and I thee pay,
　Exacted by thy fate, on the just day.

Oh, could I lose all father now! For why
　Will man lament the state he should envy?
To have so soon 'scaped world's and flesh's rage,
　And, if no other misery, yet age?
Rest in soft peace, and, asked, say here doth lie
　Ben Johnson his best piece of poetry;
For whose sake, henceforth, all his vows be such,
　As what he loves may never like too much.

Dr Robert Woof

RESOLUTION AND INDEPENDENCE
by William Wordsworth 1770–1850

There was a roaring in the wind all night;
The rain came heavily, and fell in floods;
But now the sun is rising calm and bright;
The birds are singing in the distant woods;
Over his own sweet voice the stock-dove broods;
The jay makes answer as the magpie chatters;
And all the air is fill'd with pleasant noise of water.

All things that love the sun are out of doors;
The sky rejoices in the morning's birth;
The grass is bright with rain-drops; on the moors
The hare is running races in her mirth;
And with her feet she from the plashy earth
Raises a mist; which, glittering in the sun,
Runs with her all the way, wherever she doth run.

I was a traveller then upon the moor;
I saw the hare that raced about with joy;
I heard the woods and distant waters roar,
Or heard them not, as happy as a boy:
The pleasant season did my heart employ:
My old remembrances went from me wholly;
And all the ways of men, so vain and melancholy!

But, as it sometimes chanceth, from the might
Of joy in minds that can no farther go,
As high as we have mounted in delight
In our dejection do we sink as low;
To me that morning did it happen so,
And fears and fancies thick upon me came;
Dim sadness and blind thoughts I knew not, nor could name.

I heard the skylark singing in the sky;
And I bethought me of the playful hare;
Even such a happy child of earth am I;

Even as these blissful creatures do I fare;
Far from the world I walk, and from all care;
But there may come another day to me –
Solitude, pain of heart, distress, and poverty.

My whole life I have lived in pleasant thought,
As is life's business were a summer mood;
As if all needful things would come unsought
To genial faith, still rich in genial good;
But how can he expect that others should
Build for him, sow for him, and at his call
Love him, who for himself will take no heed at all!

I thought of Chatterton, the marvellous boy,
The sleepless soul that perish'd in his pride;
Of him who walk'd in glory and in joy
Behind his plough upon the mountain side:
By our own spirits are we deified;
We poets in our youth begin in gladness;
But thereof comes in the end despondency and madness.

Now, whether it were by peculiar grace,
A leading from above, a something given,
Yet it befell, that in this lonely place,
When up and down my fancy thus was driven,
And I with these untoward thoughts had striven,
I saw a man before me unawares:
The oldest man he seem'd that ever wore grey hairs.

My course I stopp'd as soon as I espied
The old man in that naked wilderness:
Close by a pond upon the further side
He stood alone: a minute's space I guess
I watch'd him, he continued motionless:
To the pool's further margin then I drew,
He being all the while before me full in view.

As a huge stone is sometimes seen to lie
Couch'd on the bald top of an eminence,
Wonder to all who do the same espy
By what means it could thither come, and whence,
So that it seems a thing endued with sense:
Like a sea-beast crawl'd forth, which on a shelf
Of rock or sand reposeth, there to sun itself.

Such seem'd this man, not all alive nor dead,
Nor all asleep, in his extreme old age:
His body was bent double, feet and head
Coming together in their pilgrimage,
As if some dire constraint of pain, or rage
Of sickness felt by him in times long past,
A more than human weight upon his frame had cast.

Himself he propp'd, his body, limbs, and face,
Upon a long grey staff of shaven wood;
And, still as I drew near with gentle pace,
Beside the little pond or moorish flood,
Motionless as a cloud the old man stood;
That heareth not the loud winds when they call,
And moveth all together, if it move at all.

At length, himself unsettling, he the pond
Stirr'd with his staff, and fixedly did look
Upon the muddy water, which he conn'd,
As if he had been reading in a book:
And now such freedom as I could I took,
And, drawing to his side, to him did say,
'This morning gives us promise of a glorious day.'

A gentle answer did the old man make,
In courteous speech, which forth he slowly drew;
And him with further words I thus bespake:

'What kind of work is that which you pursue?
This is a lonesome place for one like you.'
He answer'd me with pleasure and surprise,
And there was, while he spake, a fire about his eyes.

His words came feebly, from a feeble chest,
Yet each in solemn order follow'd each,
With something of a lofty utterance dress'd;
Choice word, and measured phrase; above the reach
Of ordinary men; a stately speech;
Such as grave livers do in Scotland use,
Religious men, who give to God and man their dues.

He told me that he to this pond had come
To gather leeches, being old and poor.
Employment hazardous and wearisome:
And he had many hardships to endure;
From pond to pond he roam'd, from moor to moor,
Housing, with God's good help, by choice or chance;
And in this way he gain'd an honest maintenance.

The old man still stood talking by my side;
But now his voice to me was like a stream
Scarce heard, nor word from word could I divide;
And the whole body of the man did seem
Like one whom I had met with in a dream;
Or like a man from some far region sent
To give me human strength and strong admonishment.

My former thoughts return'd: the fear that kills,
And hope that is unwilling to be fed;
Cold, pain, and labour, and all fleshly ills;
And mighty poets in their misery dead.
But now, perplex'd by what the old man had said,
My question eagerly did I renew.
'How is it that you live, and what is it you do?'

He with a smile did then his words repeat;
And said, that, gathering leeches, far and wide
He travell'd; stirring thus about his feet
The waters of the ponds where they abide.
'Once I could meet with them on every side;
But they have dwindled long by slow decay;
Yet still I persevere, and find them where I may.'

While he was talking thus, the lonely place,
The old man's shape, and speech, all troubled me;
In my mind's eye I seem'd to see him pace
About the weary moors continually,
Wandering about alone and silently.
While I these thoughts within myself pursued,
He, having made a pause, the same discourse renew'd.

And soon with this he other matter blended,
Cheerfully utter'd, with demeanour kind,
But stately in the main; and when he ended,
I could have laugh'd myself to scorn, to find
In that decrepit man so firm a mind.
'God,' said I, 'be my help and stay secure;
I'll think of the leech-gatherer on the lonely moor.'

Kit Wright

SHY GEORDIE

by Helen Cruickshank 1887–1975

Up the Noran Water
  In by Inglismaddy,
Annie's got a bairnie
  That hasna got a daddy,
Some say it's Tammas's
  An' some say it's Chay's,
Yet naebody expec'it it,
  Wi' Annie's quiet ways.

Up the Noran Water
  The bonnie little mannie,
Is dandled and cuddled close,
  By Inglismaddy's Annie,
Wha' the bairnie's faither is
  The lassiue never says;
But some think it's Tammas's
  An' some think it's Chay's.

Up the Noran Water
  The country folk are kind;
An' wha' the bairnie's faither is
  They dinna muckle mind.
But oh! the bairn at Annie's breist,
  The love in Annie's e'e;
They mak' me wish wi' a' my micht
  The lucky lad was me!

Index Of First Lines

156

ACKNOWLEDGEMENTS

The publishers would like to acknowledge the following for permission to reproduce copyright material:

Oxford University Press for 'Part of Plenty' from Bernard Spencer's *Collected Poems* edited by Roger Bowen (1981); Virago Press Ltd for 'Game After Supper' © Margaret Atwood 1976; Peters, Fraser & Dunlop for 'Spirits of Movement' by James Berry from *The New British Poetry* published by Paladin; Charlotte Sheedy Literary Agency, Inc., New York for 'A Litany of Survival' © 1978 by Audre Lorde; Faber & Faber Ltd for 'The Discovery of the Pacific' from *Selected Poems 1950–75* by Thom Gunn; James MacGibbon for 'O Pug!' from *The Collected Poems of Stevie Smith* published by Penguin Twentieth Century Classics; Faber & Faber Ltd for 'MCMXIV' from *The Whitsun Weddings* by Philip Larkin; Dorothea Carberry for 'Nature' by H. D. Carberry; Joy Scott, executor of the Estate of Dennis Scott for 'Marrysong' from *Strategies* by Dennis Scott; Reed Book Services for 'At a Warwickshire Mansion' from *New and Collected Poems* © 1985 Roy Fuller, published by Martin Secker & Warburg Ltd; Oxford University Press for 'For Andrew' from Fleur Adcock's *Selected Poems*; New Directions Publishing Corporation for the translation by Stephen Spender and J. L. Gili of 'The Faithless Wife' from *The Selected Poems of Federico Garcia Lorca*; Gwilym R. Jones for his poem 'Salm I'r Creaduriaid' (Psalm to the Creatures); Ebenezer Morris for the extract from 'Gwalia Deserta' by Idris Davies; Peters, Fraser & Dunlop for 'Three Poets Play the Saké Cup Game' from *Unplayed Music* by Carol Rumens published by Martin Secker & Warburg Ltd; Faber & Faber Ltd for 'The Oak and The Olive' from *Collected Poems* by George Barker; Faber & Faber Ltd for 'The Forge' from *Door into the Dark* by Seamus Heaney; New Beacon Books Ltd for 'Heartease New England 1987' from *Heartease* by Lorna Goodison (1988); Oxford University Press for 'Paraphrases' from *Poems 1955–87* by Roy Fisher (1988); David McDuff for his translation of 'I Have the Present of a Body' by Osip Mandelstam; Carcanet Press Ltd for Stephen Conn's translation of 'Going Blind' by Rainer Maria Rilke; The Gallery Press for 'The Pleasant Joys of Brotherhood' from *Poems 1956–86* by James Simmons; David Higham Associates for 'Autobiography' from *Collected Poems* by Louis MacNeice published by Faber & Faber Ltd; Peterloo Poets for 'Thoughts After Ruskin' by Elma Mitchell; W. D. Snodgrass for his poem 'Lobsters in the Window'; Farrar, Straus & Giroux, Inc. for 'Cirque d'Hiver' from *The Complete Poems 1927–79* by Elizabeth Bishop; Faber & Faber Ltd for 'Life, Friends, Is Boring' from *The Dream Songs* by John Berryman; G. Thomas for 'Pilgrimages' by R. S. Thomas; David Higham Associates for the extract from 'Santa Claus' from *Bell Harry* by

Christopher Hassall, published by Longmans; Mrs Nessie Graham for 'Enter A Cloud' © the Estate of W. S. Graham; Faber & Faber Ltd for 'The Fox' from *Meeting the British* by Paul Muldoon; Faber & Faber Ltd for 'Rose' from *Fifty Poems* by Ian Hamilton; Faber & Faber Ltd for 'Song' from *Collected Poems* by Edwin Muir; Morton L. Leavy for 'Telephone Conversation' by Wole Soyinka; Nigel Forde for his poem 'And Some of the Larger Pieces That You See Are Called Uncles'; Faber & Faber Ltd for 'To Speak of the Woe That is in Marriage' from *Life Studies* by Robert Lowell; The Gallery Press and the Trustees of the Estate of Patrick Kavanagh for his poem 'Innocence'; Random Century for 'Stopping by Woods on a Snowy Evening' from *The Poetry of Robert Frost* edited by Edward Connery Lathem, published by Jonathan Cape; Virago Press Ltd for 'Caged Bird' by Maya Angelou; Faber & Faber Ltd for 'Reference Rock' from *The Whitsun Weddings* by Philip Larkin; James MacGibbon for 'Thoughts About the Person from Porlock' from *The Collected Poems of Stevie Smith* published by Penguin Twentieth Century Classics; Random Century for 'Design' from *The Poetry of Robert Frost* edited by Edward Connery Lathem, published by Jonathan Cape; Angus & Robertson Bay Books for 'Terra Australis' from *Collected Poems* by James McAuley, © Norma McAuley; HarperCollins Publishers for the translation by Stanley Kunitz with Max Hayward of 'Lot's Wife' by Anna Akhmatova; the E. E. Cummings Trust and George J. Firmage for 'Buffalo Bill 's' by E. E. Cummings; The Literary Trustrees of Walter de la Mare and The Society of Authors as their representative for 'Fare Well'; Raymond Garlick for his poem 'The Sisters' from *Collected Poems 1946–86* published by Gwasg Gomer (1987); David Higham Associates for 'Snow' from *Collected Poems* by Louis MacNeice published by Faber & Faber Ltd; The E. E. Cummings Trust and George J. Firmage for 'anyone lived in a pretty how town' by E. E. Cummings; A. C. Hunter for 'Shy Geordie' by Helen Cruickshank.

The Publishers have made every effort to trace copyright holders of material reproduced within this compilation. If, however, they have inadvertently made any error they would be grateful for notification.